PUBLICATIONS BY LEONID OUSPENSKY
AVAILABLE FROM ST VLADIMIR'S SEMINARY PRESS

The Meaning of Icons

Theology of the Icon, Volumes 1 & 2

PATRICK DOOLAN

Recovering the Icon

The Life & Work of
Leonid Ouspensky

Foreword by Anthony Bloom, Metropolitan of Sourozh

Biography by Lydia Ouspensky

ST VLADIMIR'S SEMINARY PRESS
CRESTWOOD, NEW YORK · 2008

This book is dedicated to:
Lydia Alexandrevna Ouspensky

For their contributions to this book, we thank:

Gregory Aslanov
Katherine Aslanov
Anne Headley
Mariamna Fortounatto
George Koregelos
M. Mihalick
Helena Nikkannen
Jean-Claude Larchet

Library of Congress Cataloging-in-Publication Data

Doolan, Patrick.
    [Redécouverte de l'icone. English]
    Recovering the icon : the life & work of Leonid Ouspensky / Patrick Doolan;
foreword by Antony Bloom ; Metropolitan of Sourozh biography by Lydia Ouspensky.
— 1st English language ed.
        p.   cm.
    Includes bibliographical references.
    ISBN 0–88141–270–8 (978–0–88141–270–3 : alk. paper)
   1. Ouspensky, Léonide—Catalogs.   2. Icons, Russian—France—20th century—
Catalogs.   I. Ouspensky, Léonide.   II. Title.

N8189.5.O96A4 2008
704.9'482092—dc22

                                2008006149

Copyright © 2008 by

ST VLADIMIR'S SEMINARY PRESS
575 Scarsdale Rd, Crestwood, NY 10707
1–800–204–2665
www.svspress.com

All photographs © 2001 Patrick Doolan

Originally published in French as *La Redécouverte de l'icône:*
La vie et l'oeuvre de Léonide Ouspensky (Paris: Les Éditions du Cerf, copyright 2001).

Cover and book design: Amber Schley

ISBN 978–0–88141–270–3

PRINTED IN CHINA

Contents

List of Plates

Foreword

Three men, we are told in the *Life* of one of the Desert Dwellers of old, came to see a hermit renowned for his wisdom. Two of them asked him questions which no one had hitherto been able to answer; the third visitor sat in silence.

At the end of this encounter the Old Man said to the one who had sat, silent, all the time: "Brother, why didst thou ask no question?"

"It was enough for me to look at thee," replied the man.

Leonid Ouspensky was a man of not many words, but he had a presence which was sufficient for one to commune with him.

I met him for the first time when I was seventeen years old. We stood a few yards apart in the same church until I left France, a priest of thirty-five years of age. In all these years we had never talked—we had been present to one another, communing silently through prayer in the various services we both attended; we never tried to reach out to one another; we stood there, together, in God's Presence, meeting him and, therefore, one another.

What impressed me in Ouspensky was the quiet collectedness of all his person: he neither recoiled from you nor ever moved into your inner space. Total, unaffected stillness is what I remember when I think of him. And you could read him, revealed, in the icons he painted. For him an icon was the projection in line and colors of an experience of things eternal; an experience that was personal: that of a person, a living member of the mysterious Body of Christ, not of a separate individual projecting, as it were, himself for others to see and admire. Through the person it was (as it should be) the experience of the whole Body, the Church, that reached one.

An icon was not to him an aesthetic creation but a vision in lines and colors of the Divine world, and it pervaded, conquered, transfigured the fallen world. It is only by looking deeply, in the silence of contemplation, that one can enter into the spiritual world of Ouspensky, because it found expression in the terms of this world, both fallen and redeemed, both wrapped in twilight and at the same time pervaded by the Light of God.

If you want to know Ouspensky, stand in silence for a long while before an icon of his and receive the message that will allow you to commune with the contemplative silence out of which—within which—it was born, and the ardent faith which made him one who reveals to the world its true vocation and, indeed, its true nature.

Metropolitan Anthony of Sourozh

LEONID ALEXANDROVICH OUSPENSKY, 1902–1987

Ouspensky, at work in his studio, where he lived with his wife,
Lydia Alexandrevna, at 39, rue Breguet, Paris, France

THE WORK OF
LEONID OUSPENSKY

The Work of Leonid Ouspensky

This iconostasis[1] is in the parish church of Our Lady, Joy of All Who Sorrow and St Geneviève of Paris, located in rue Saint-Victor in Paris. The parish was founded in 1935 for French-speaking people, under the Patriarchate of Moscow. The parish has been at the present site since 1965. In converting a preexisting secular space to the sacred space of the Divine Liturgy, the parish followed in the steps of the early Church, which often modified secular buildings for liturgical use.[2] Ouspensky designed the iconostasis for the church in rue Saint-Victor. He painted the icons and carved the cherubim beneath the principal icons. The structure is simple and elegant, giving focus and prominence to the icons and not distracting the attention of the congregation with superfluous detail or ornament. The lines in the design of the iconostasis lead the eye to the white-clad figure of the Enthroned Christ, who sits among the saints in the top row of icons, his hand raised in blessing. To the right of Christ: St John the Forerunner; the Archangel Gabriel; St Paul the Apostle; St John Chrysostom; St Irenaeus of Lyons; St Seraphim of Sarov; and St Demetrios the Great Martyr. To the left of Christ: the Virgin Mary; the Archangel Michael; St Peter the Apostle; St Dionysios the Areopagite; St Sergius of Radonezh; St Victor the Martyr. This range of icons corresponds very closely to a description left to us by St Symeon of Thessalonica writing in the fourteenth century:

> . . . the columns are joined by an unbroken decorated architrave signifying the bond of charity, which is the communion in Christ between earthly saints and heavenly beings. This is why a

picture of the Savior is placed here in the middle of the sacred images. His Mother and the Baptist are on either side of him with angels and Archangels, the apostles and the rest of the saints. This signifies Christ in heaven with his saints, Christ as he is with us now and Christ who will come again.[3]

At the top of the archway, above the Royal Doors (the central opening leading into the sanctuary), is a small icon of the Holy Trinity. To either side of this arch, on two panels that curve out from the feet of the enthroned Savior, is the icon of the Communion of the Apostles, emphasizing Christ's role as High Priest, and furthering the eucharistic expression of the iconostasis. As the faithful stand before this arch to receive communion, they look up and see that they are doing so among the apostles themselves.

The Royal Doors contain icons of the Annunciation, and the four Evangelists—Matthew, Mark, Luke, and John. To either side of these are the icons of Christ and the Mother of God, designed as full-stature standing figures, making appropriate use of the available space, and presenting the worshipper with an intimate yet monumental vision of God made man.

In the following 11 pages, the various icons of the ensemble will be examined, but looking at the whole iconostasis pictured here, one may note that the design itself is one of Leonid Ouspensky's great works, utilizing the concise and laconic artistic language of traditional Orthodox iconography, and showing the function and meaning of the icon with the humility and clarity that typified his life and work.

---

1 Cf. "The Problem of the Iconostasis," by Leonid Ouspensky, *St Vladimir's Seminary Quarterly* 8.4 (1964): 186–218.

2 The earliest known example is the early third-century *domus ecclesiae* ("house church"=Latin) discovered among the ruins of the ancient town of Dura Europos, excavated in 1921 in present-day Syria. See C. Bradford Welles, *The Excavations at Dura-Europos,* Part II (New Haven, CT: Dura-Europos Publications), distributed by J.J. Augustin Publisher, Locust Valley, NY, 1967. St Luke notes the existence of Christians meeting in converted homes in Acts 20:7–8.

3 Symeon Thessalonicensis, *De Sacro Templo*, Patrologia Graeca, ed. J.-P. Migne, col. 155, 305–362.

Plate 1 ICONOSTASIS
Height: 390 cm x 303 cm
Church of Our Lady, Joy of All Who Sorrow and St Geneviève of Paris,
Rue Saint-Victor, Paris, 1968

Plate 2 ICONOSTASIS
Church of Our Lady, Joy of All Who Sorrow and
St Geneviève of Paris, rue Saint-Victor, Paris

Christ is seen over the Royal Doors with the Virgin (left) and St John the Forerunner (right) in an attitude of intercession. Christ is seated on a transparent throne painted within a blue mandorla[4] superimposed on a red, four-pointed star. Transparent renderings of cherubim and seraphim are visible within the mandorla. The imagery has a scriptural basis:

> After this I looked, and behold, a door was opened in heaven; and the first voice which I heard was, as it were, of a trumpet talking with me which said, Come up hither, and I will show thee things which must be hereafter. And immediately I was in the Spirit; and behold, a throne was set in Heaven, and One sat on the throne. And he that sat thereon was to look upon like a jasper and a sardine stone; and there was a rainbow round about the throne, in sight like unto an emerald.[5]

Within the four corners of the red four-pointed star are shown four winged figures, the symbols of the four Evangelists—Matthew (represented by a angel, upper left), Mark (the Lion, lower left), Luke (the Bull, lower right) and John (the Eagle, upper right). Like the cherubim and seraphim they are rendered transparent.

Again, the iconography is taken from Scripture:

> and before the throne there was a sea of glass like unto crystal. And in the midst of the throne, and round about the throne, were four beasts full of eyes before and behind. And the first beast was like a lion, and the second beast like a calf, and the third beast had a face as a man, and the fourth beast was like a flying eagle. And the four beasts had each of them six wings about him; and they were full of eyes within; and they rest not day and night, saying, Holy, holy, holy, Lord God Almighty, which was, and is, and is to come. And when those beasts give glory and honor and thanks to him that sat on the throne, who liveth for ever and ever. . . .[6]

Christ is shown in shining white garments, holding an open Gospel with the text, "I am the Way, the Truth and the Life."[7] The depiction of the Deisis in this position over the Royal Doors had fallen out of use in Orthodox churches by the end of the nineteenth century, and was often replaced by the Last Supper. Ouspensky advocated the restoration of the older tradition,[8] citing fundamental early texts from Paul the Silentiary[9] and St Symeon of Thessalonica.[10]

4 The almond-shaped aureole, or halo, surrounds figures which are sources of divine light—usually Christ himself. Cf. "Mandorla," *The Oxford Companion to Art*, ed. Harold Osborne (Oxford University Press, 1970), 684–85.

5 Rev 4:1–3.

6 Rev 4: 6–9.

7 Mt 14:6.

8 "The Problem of the Iconostasis," 186–218.

9 Paulus Silentiarius, *Descriptio Sanctae Sophiae et Anbonis*, ed. I. Sekker, Bonn 1837. Cf. Cyril Mango, *The Art of the Byzantine Empire* 312–1453 (Toronto: Sources and Documents, 1986), 87–88.

10 *De Sacro Templo* 136, MPG, clv, col. 345.

Plate 3 Detail: THE DEISIS OVER THE ROYAL DOORS (Plate 1)
Height: 56 cm x 90 cm (approx.)
Iconostasis, Church of Our Lady, Joy of All Who Sorrow and St Geneviève of Paris, rue Saint-Victor, Paris, 1968
Egg tempera on gessoed wood

Plate 4 Detail: CHRIST THE SAVIOR (Plate 6)

Plates 5 and 6 Detail: THE VIRGIN HODIGITRIA, CHRIST THE SAVIOR (Plate 1)
Each panel: 92.5 cm x 38 cm
Iconostasis, Church of Our Lady, Joy of All Who Sorrow and St Geneviève of Paris, rue Saint-Victor, Paris, 1968
Egg tempera on gessoed wood

Plate 7 Detail: THE COMMUNION OF THE APOSTLES (Plate 1)
Height: 56 cm x 56.6 cm
Iconostasis, Church of Our Lady, Joy of All Who Sorrow and St Geneviève of Paris, rue Saint-Victor, Paris, 1968
Egg tempera on gessoed wood

Plate 8 ICONOSTASIS
Church of Our Lady, Joy of All Who Sorrow and St Geneviève of
Paris, rue Saint-Victor, Paris

Plate 9 Detail: THE COMMUNION OF THE APOSTLES (Plate 1)

Plate 10 Detail: THE COMMUNION OF THE APOSTLES (Plate 1)
Height: 56 cm x 56.6 cm
Iconostasis, Church of Our Lady, Joy of All Who Sorrow and St Geneviève of Paris, rue Saint-Victor, Paris, 1968
Egg tempera on gessoed wood

The Communion of the Apostles is presented in two parts above and to either side of the Royal Doors. Christ is depicted twice (both left and right), administering the Communion of his Blood (right) and of his Body (left) to two groups of six apostles, led by SS Peter (left) and Paul (right). Christ is standing behind an Altar Table which is vested in a red cloth with gold trim and white crosses. In each depiction, Christ stands in front of a throne reminiscent of the Bishop's seat found in the same position in Orthodox churches. The apostles approach Communion in attitudes of eager reverence. The members of the congregation are reminded that as they approach Communion, they follow in the apostles' footsteps. This icon is a liturgical interpretation of the Mystical Supper—hence the inclusion of St Paul—not present historically at the Mystical Supper, but present here to indicate the fullness of the Church. Since this icon is positioned at the gates to the sanctuary, where the laity receive Holy Communion, its presence reinforces the dogmatic meaning of the icon and underlines the eucharistic theme of the entire iconostasis.

Plate 11
Detail: THE ROYAL DOORS (Plate 12)

The doors are constructed of wood, serving as a frame with openings for the six icons, which are separately inserted from the back. The shape of the doors echoes the shape of the traditional domed Eastern Orthodox church. In the curved, dome-shaped space at the top, the Annunciation is shown on two separate panels, (the Virgin Mary, right, the Archangel Gabriel, left). Both figures lean forward at the moment which brings heaven and earth together.[11] The Archangel raises his hand in a gesture that denotes annunciation and benediction: "Hail, thou that art highly favored, the Lord is with thee: blessed art thou among women."[12] The Virgin Mary's gesture signals her acceptance of the Archangel's message, and her acceptance to bear God in the flesh: "Behold the handmaid of the Lord; be it unto me according to thy word."[13] Above her, a section of a sphere is visible, which is the iconographic sign indicating the heavens opening. The Holy Spirit overshadows her in the form of three rays that denote the energies of the Holy Trinity.

Below the Annunciation, the four Evangelists are presented, arranged in the same order in which their Gospels appear in the New Testament. Beginning with the upper right, moving clockwise around the doors: SS Matthew, Mark, Luke, and John the Theologian. Each of the four Evangelists is depicted in the act of writing the Gospel that bears his name. On each book the opening words of each Gospel are written. The icons of SS Matthew, Mark, and Luke share a similar compositional scheme. In each, the evangelist sits on a low stool at a writing desk, his head framed within the white background area formed by the spaces between the buildings. As he bends intently forward over the open Gospel book, the curving contour of his back contrasts dramatically with the angular buildings. The painter allows the contour of the figure to lead the eye of the viewer to the face of the saint, with its calm expression of inner concentration.

The icon of St John has a different composition and setting: the Theologian sits in a desert cave[14] looking intently up over his right shoulder, where part of a sphere is shown, from which three transparent rays emanate, symbolizing the activity of the Holy Trinity. In this manner the writings of the Apostle John are shown to be a revelation which he communicates to his disciple Prochoros, who transcribes the words of the Gospel.

11 Lk 1:26–38.

12 Lk 1:28.

13 Lk 1:38.

14 Rev 1:9.

Plate 12 Detail: THE ROYAL DOORS (Plate 1)
199 cm x 88 cm
Iconostasis, Church of Our Lady, Joy of All Who Sorrow and St Geneviève of Paris, rue Saint-Victor, Paris, 1968
Egg tempera on gessoed wood

Plate 13 Detail: Saint John the Evangelist with His Disciple Saint Prochoros (Plate 12)
35 cm x 30 cm
Royal Doors, Iconostasis, Church of Our Lady, Joy of All Who Sorrow and St Geneviève of Paris, rue Saint-Victor, Paris, 1968
Egg tempera on gessoed wood

Plate 14 Detail: Saint Luke the Evangelist (Plate 12)
35 cm x 30 cm
Royal Doors, Iconostasis, Church of Our Lady, Joy of All Who Sorrow and St Geneviève of Paris, rue Saint-Victor, Paris, 1968
Egg tempera on gessoed wood

Plate 15 CHRIST THE SAVIOR
27.5 cm x 18 cm
Private collection of Mme L. Ouspensky
Egg tempera on gessoed wood

Plate 16 CHRIST THE SAVIOR
24.2 cm x 19.5 cm
Private collection of J.-C. and A. Larchet, 1973
Egg tempera on gessoed wood

On this page we see two icons of Christ, shown from the shoulders up, wearing a deep blue *himation* over a dark red tunic. On either side of his halo can be seen the Greek abbreviation IC XC ("Jesus Christ"). Within the halo is a Cross with the Greek letters O WN ("He Who Is")—the divine name revealed to Moses on Sinai[15] inscribed in the three visible arms. The Savior's penetrating gaze is aimed directly at the viewer; the face is concentrated, serious, and challenging. In spite of the clear similarities between the two icons, there are differences, demonstrating the creativity of the iconographer in painting the same iconographic subject more than once. The first icon, on the left, with its gold leaf halo, has warm, subtle colors, delicately contrasted, giving the icon a somber, rich tonality, with the head of the Savior turning slightly towards the viewer. The second icon, on the right, with its olive green halo, has more varied colors, deeper contrasts, and bold, frontal presentation. Ouspensky exemplifies what can be observed in any collection of ancient, traditional icons: the artistic abilities of the painter are always fully engaged. We will see the familiar face of the Lord in icon after icon, but these icons will never be identical.

15 Ex 3:14.

Plate 17 THE SAVIOR ACHEIROPOIETOS
25.5 cm x 19 cm
Private collection of P. Forstmann
Egg tempera on gessoed wood

Plate 18 THE SAVIOR ACHEIROPOIETOS
28 cm x 20.6 cm
Private collection of J.-C. and A. Larchet
Egg tempera on gessoed wood

Acheiropoietos is the Greek term for "not made by hands," referring to the origin of this icon type: Christ pressed a towel to his face, leaving an image on the fabric. This icon is alternatively known as "The Mandylion" (napkin=Greek) and also as "The Holy Face." This icon's feast is celebrated on August 16.[16] The Savior's face is emblazoned on a white cloth trimmed in red. Natural earth tones predominate in both icons shown here, which successfully combines great calm with intense power, above all in the concentrated expression of the eyes and brows. This icon type has had a particularly rich history in the Church. The *mandylion* on which Christ left the image of his face was taken to the trading city of Edessa where its king, Abgar, held it in great veneration. After a complex sequence of events—including its being walled up to protect it from Persian invaders, and its miraculous rediscovery—the Holy Face was taken to Constantinople, where it remained in the imperial palace as one of the city's great sacred treasures. It was looted in AD 1204 by Western soldiers during the disastrous Fourth Crusade, and taken to Western Europe. Its subsequent history has been complicated by its association with the famous Shroud of Turin—a link Ouspensky and many others found spurious. The *mandylion* depicts a living face with open eyes; the Turin Shroud depicts a corpse with a dead face. Copies of the *Acheiropoietos* have always been among the most popular and widespread throughout the Christian East and remain so today.

16 See Hieromonk Makarios of Simonos Petra, "*L'image non faite de main d'homme,*" *The Synaxarion,* Tome 5 (Thessalonica: Editions To Perivoli tis Panaghias, 1996), 426–429; St Nikolai Velimirovic, "The Icon of our Lord Jesus Christ Not-made-with-hands," in *The Prologue from Ochrid,* Part Three, (Birmingham, England: Lazarica Press, 1986), 201; Leonid Ouspensky, *The Theology of the Icon* Vol. 1 (Crestwood, NY: St Vladimir's Seminary Press, 1978), 51–58.

Other examples of CHRIST IN GLORY (from left: Plates 100, 3, 85)

Opposite: Plate 19 CHRIST IN GLORY
Private collection, J. van Ael, 1984
Egg tempera on gessoed linden wood

In Plate 19 (p. 31), Christ is depicted in a white robe with a gold *clavus*,[17] his right hand raised in blessing, his left supporting a Gospel book open to the text, "I am the Way, the Truth, and the Life."[18] He sits in the midst of a dark blue mandorla, in which appear luminous six-winged cherubim (the winged faces) and many-eyed seraphim (the winged circles of eyes to the left and right of the footstool). At the four corners of the panel appear (clockwise from top left) the Angel, Eagle, Bull, and Lion that stand for the four Evangelists, Matthew, John, Luke, and Mark.[19] The iconography of the icon of Christ in Glory has been examined in the description of the Deisis icon (plate 3, p. 19).

Ouspensky always taught that the ancient icons themselves are the best teachers for learning iconography, and exhorted his students to pay close attention to the manner in which each area of paint was applied to the panel, as well as to the relation among the colors of the icon. This particular icon makes great use of the color white, and even the empty background shapes play an important role in the composition. A yellowish raw

sienna base color is covered over with white paint, but not so as to hide the underlying layer entirely. As a result, these spaces have a life and strength to them, and appear to be permeated with the light that emanates from the Savior. The light of Christ appears to engulf and illumine the symbolic figures of the four Evangelists, who in turn themselves becomes bearers of light, as they carry their Gospels from him to the ends of the earth. Thus, Christ is shown to be the source of light that comes into the world:

> For God, who commanded the light to shine out
> of darkness, hath shined in our hearts, to give the
> light of the knowledge of the glory of God in the
> face of Jesus Christ.[20]

The icon reproduced here can be compared with three other icons of Christ in Glory, pictured above, where the same iconographic subject is rendered in different media (for larger reproductions and explanatory texts, see Plates 3, 85, and 100).

17 *Clavus*: A colored band on the tunic, running from the shoulder to the bottom hem of the tunic, a sign of distinction, and signifying the function of a messenger. It is found on the tunic of Christ, the angels, the prophets, and the apostles.

18 Jn 14:6.

19 Rev 4:9.

20 2 Cor 4:6.

СТА҃ТРОНЦА

Plate 20 THE HOLY TRINITY
31 cm x 24.3 cm
Church of the Three Hierarchs, rue Petel, Paris, circa 1960
Egg tempera on gessoed wood

Tradition of the Church is always foremost in Ouspensky's icons; indeed, it is one of the hallmarks of his work:

> Therefore the Church has repeatedly emphasized the necessity to follow the Tradition, either through rulings of councils, or through the voice of its dignitaries, and enjoined that icons would be painted "as the ancient holy iconographers painted them."[21]

The appearance of the Three Mysterious Visitors to Abraham and Sarah recounted in Genesis 18 is taken by the Christian Fathers as a reference to the Holy Trinity. The icon often includes Abraham and Sarah, making plain the connection to the visitation (in such a case, the icon is called, "The Hospitality of Abraham and Sarah"). Here, the reference is succinctly reduced to the Oak of Mamre rising between the angels, the dwelling of Abraham and Sarah in the background, and the table set by them in the midst of the angels. The usual identification is, from left to right, Father, Son, and Holy Spirit. The angels sit on a raised platform around a central table or altar. Each angelic Being extends his right hand, blessing a cup containing the head of a sacrificed animal, signifying the voluntary passion and death of Christ. The architectural rendering to the left references the site as a place of human habitation, faithful to the Genesis account.

The two icons shown here are interesting for both the similarities and differences in the artistic execution. The composition of the two are very much alike, each based on the celebrated icon of the Holy Trinity by St Andrei Rublev. Extreme faithfulness to the iconographic

The differences between the icons lie chiefly in their colors. The Icon to the left has a very warm color palette, dominated by rather solid yellows and golds; that to the right has a palette of translucent blues and purples. Together they demonstrate the manner in which Ouspensky utilized old icons as the models for his own work:

> Iconography, therefore is not copying, it is far from being impersonal, for to follow Tradition never shackles the creative powers of the iconographer, whose individuality expresses itself in the composition as well as the color and line. But the personal is here much more subtle than in other arts and so often escapes superficial observation. The absence of identical icons has been noted long ago. Indeed among icons on the same subject, although they are sometimes remarkably alike, we never find two identical icons (except in cases of deliberate copying in more modern times). Icons are not copied but are "painted from," which signifies a free and creative transposition. [22]

21 Leonid Ouspensky, *The Meaning of Icons* (Crestwood, NY: St Vladimir's Seminary Press, 1989), 42.

22 Ibid., 43.

LA SAINTE TRINITE

Plate 21 THE HOLY TRINITY
27.4 cm x 21.7 cm
Private collection of J.-C. and A. Larchet, 1977
Egg tempera on gessoed wood

Plate 22 THE VIRGIN OF THE SIGN
25 cm x 19 cm
Private collection of P. Forstmann
1976
Egg tempera on gessoed wood

Therefore the Lord himself shall give you a sign;
Behold, a virgin shall conceive, and bear a son, and
shall call his name Emmanuel.[23]

The icon on the facing page (plate 23, p. 35) depicts the
Savior within a mandorla in front of the Virgin, in a
white tunic and robe with a bright red clavus. He holds
a scroll in his left hand, his right hand raised in blessing.
The mandorla is, at the center, deep blue-green, with an
outer circle of lighter green. Beneath her warm purple
maforion, the Virgin wears a sea green tunic. Two six-
winged cherubim are depicted on each side of the Virgin, a visual reminder of her status as "more honorable
than the cherubim and beyond compare more glorious
than the seraphim," in the words of a familiar Orthodox

hymn. Her hands are raised in
prayer to her divine Son. Her
sleeves are covered in white
highlights, which reflect light
emanating from the Child
himself, who has as one of his
most frequent liturgical titles,
"Christ the true light that
enlighteneth every man coming into the world."

This large icon, one of the
largest panel icons Ouspensky ever painted, hangs on the
east wall of the sanctuary of
the Church of Our Lady, Joy
of All Who Sorrow and St Geneviève in Paris (see the
icon screen of this church, plate 1, p. 17). The icon pictured above (plate 22) is of the same subject, but is a
small icon that is meant to hang in the icon corner of an
individual's home. It shows several variations: The background is bright red, and the gesture of blessing is different, as he blesses with both hands. There is an intimacy
here which contrasts with the monumentality of the
larger icon.

The Russian title for this icon is *Znamenskaya*,
meaning, "Our Lady of the Sign," referring to Isaiah's
prophecy. The Greek name for this icon is *Platytera ton
Ouranon*, which means "She who is wider than the
Heavens," as she contained within her womb he whom
the heavens could not contain.

23 Is 7:1.

Plate 23 THE VIRGIN OF THE SIGN
100.5 cm x 79.6 cm
East Wall, Church of Our Lady, Joy of All Who Sorrow and St Geneviève of Paris, rue Saint-Victor, Paris, 1972
Egg tempera on gessoed wood

Plate 24 THE VLADIMIR MOTHER OF GOD
23 cm x 19 cm
Private collection of N. Lossky

Vladimir, from which this icon takes its name, was one of the important medieval centers of Russian life and culture before the consolidation of the nation under the leadership of Moscow.[24] It is a version of the older Byzantine icon type known as *Eleousa*, which in Greek means "merciful", while the Russian name for this type of icon is *Umilyeniye*, or "loving-kindness": where the faces of Mother and Child are gently pressed together. The Savior is depicted clad in a gold-highlighted red robe, affectionately embracing his Mother. His gaze is directed at her, and he is held in her right hand. Her left hand directs us towards him. Note the placement of the arm of the Savior (in both icons) and how the gold trim of the robe of the mother comes out of the gesture of the arm and continues all around her head, bringing our eyes to rest in the quiet and tender moment between the Virgin and her Son as their faces touch. The painter succeeds in portraying the human love between Mother and

24 G. Vernadsky, *A History of Russia* (New Haven, CT: Yale University Press, 1943).

36

Plate 25 THE VLADIMIR MOTHER OF GOD
25 cm x 17 cm
Private collection of M. Berg; Egg tempera on gessoed wood

Child with an intensity from which sentimentality is absent. This type of icon is closely associated with Russian iconography, but the origin of this icon is itself Greek and its most famous exemplar—the much-reproduced "Our Lady of Vladimir"—was painted in Constantinople. In fact, no substantive distinction can be made between Greek and Russian, or any other national form, of iconography. Rather, within each national culture, eras of greater faithfulness to the Church's actual Tradi-tion are succeeded by eras of drifting away from that standard of faithfulness. It was Ouspensky's task, work-ing within the Russian emigration in Paris, to recover the authentic norms required for any serious iconography; in this he was working against a long period of "Western captivity" of iconography following, in Russia, the imposition of Western artistic canons and taste on the Russian Church, especially during and after the reign of Catherine II (†1796).

Plate 26 THE VIRGIN OF KAZAN
28 cm x 22 cm
Private collection of J.-C. and A. Larchet
Egg tempera on gessoed linden wood

Plate 27 The Virgin of Korsun (Cherson)
8.7 cm x 6.2 cm
Private collection of G. and A. Schittly, 1984
Egg tempera on gessoed linden wood

Plates 28, 29, and 30 THE CHAPEL OF SAINT SERAPHIM OF SAROV, Patmos, Greece

above, Plate 28 The chapel and chapel garden seen from the east.
top right, Plate 29 The chapel viewed from the west. The stone structure in the background is the Monastery of St John the Evangelist.
bottom right, Plate 30 The iconostasis of the chapel.

St Seraphim died in 1833 and was canonized in 1903.[25] His feast is celebrated on January 2 and July 19. He is depicted here in a dark brown monastic *rason* (a wide-sleeved outer garment), wearing an *epitrahelion* (a long, narrow cloth worn by priests over the neck and hanging down in front full length), holding a Gospel in his covered left hand, his right hand raised in blessing. He wears the traditional monastic headgear—a cylindrical hat called a *kamilavka,* covered with a black veil, or *epikamilavkion.* This icon was commissioned for the Chapel of St Seraphim on the island of Patmos, and its inscription is in Greek.

This icon is one of the finest of St Seraphim that has come down to us. The gaze, posture, and gesture are bold and intently focused, all indicated with lines of astonishing simplicity. The icon lacks any hint of sentimentality, contrasting sharply with westernized versions of this icon popular earlier in the twentieth century. It is a good example of the way Ouspensky worked to restore the integrity of the icon in the face of the overwhelming popularity of debased religious painting. Color, contour, expression, and line are all simplified and boldly rendered, resulting in a work of intense, sober joy that forms a visual counterpart to the verbal sobriety and joy of the liturgical hymnology of the Church.

25 For a biography in English, see Valentine Zander, *St Seraphim of Sarov* (Crestwood, NY: St Vladimir's Seminary Press,, 1975) and Constantine Cavarnos and M. Zeldin, *St Seraphim of Sarov* (Belmont, MA: Institute for Byzantine and Modern Greek Studies, 1993).

Plate 31 Detail: SAINT SERAPHIM OF SAROV (Plate 30)
50 cm x 40 cm
Chapel of St Seraphim of Sarov, Patmos, Greece, 1984
Egg tempera on gessoed wood

41

Plate 32 Detail: THE VIRGIN ELEOUSA (Plate 30)
50 cm x 40 cm
Chapel of St Seraphim of Sarov, Patmos, Greece, 1984
Egg tempera on gessoed linden wood

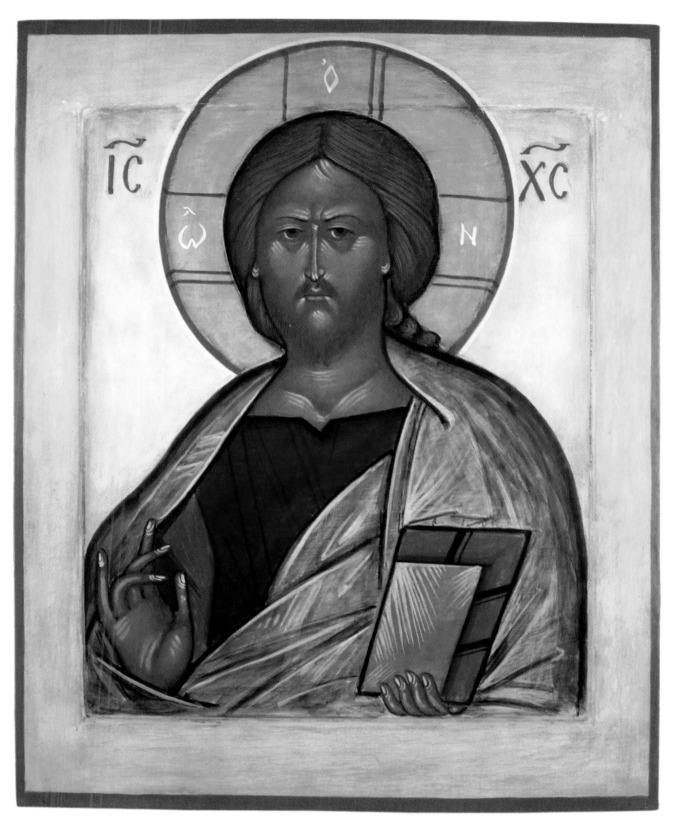

Plate 33 Detail: Christ with Open Gospel Book (Plate 30)
50 cm x 40 cm
Chapel of St Seraphim of Sarov, Patmos, Greece, 1984
Egg tempera on gessoed linden wood

Plate 34 Detail: The Virgin Eleousa (Plate 32)

Plate 35 Detail: CHRIST WITH OPEN GOSPEL BOOK (Plate 33)

Plates 36–41 Detail: DEISIS AND FESTAL ICONS (Plate 42)
Each panel: 25 cm x 18.2 cm, Church of SS Gregory and Anastasia, Bernweiller, France, 1985–1986
Plate 36: THE VIRGIN MARY; Plate 37: JESUS CHRIST; Plate 38: ST JOHN THE BAPTIST (from top left)
Plate 39: THEOPHANY; Plate 40: THE TRANSFIGURATION; Plate 41: THE ENTRY INTO JERUSALEM (from bottom left)

The church of SS Gregory and Anastasia and its iconostasis were built in 1980, according to a traditional Byzantine plan. After being asked to make the range of festal icons for the icon screen, Ouspensky himself asked if there was to be a Deisis above the Royal Doors. When he was told that there were no plans for this all-important icon, he replied that it was necessary to have the Deisis, and that without one, he would not paint any of the other icons. Those who had commissioned the icons happily received this directive from the old master and gladly added the Deisis to their plans, asking Ouspensky to paint it, along with the festal panels over the course of the following years (1985–86). These icons comprised the last large ensemble of icons that Ouspensky would paint for

any church. On the top of the iconostasis are the three first icons of the Deisis: Christ, the Virgin, and the Forerunner (St John the Baptist). The feasts are arranged in the order in which they are celebrated during the Orthodox church year: the Nativity of the Mother of God, the Elevation of the Holy Cross, the Presentation of the Mother of God to the Temple, the Nativity of Christ, Theophany, the Presentation of Christ to the Temple, the Annunciation, the Entry into Jerusalem, the Resurrection, the Ascension, Pentecost, the Transfiguration, and the Dormition of the Mother of God. Each festal icon can be easily removed, in order to set it out in the midst of the church on the day of its celebration. The colors of this ensemble of icons are remarkable for their lightness and

Plate 42 IconoStasis: DeiSis and the Range of Festal Icons
Church of SS Gregory and Anastasia, Bernweiller, France, 1985–1986

purity, and demonstrated Ouspensky's undiminished skill at putting to use beautiful color in the service of icon painting. Three of the festal panels, along with the Deisis, are shown on the page 46 (plates 36–41). In the three festal icons shown, one may note that the inscriptions are written in three languages (French, Greek, and Alsacian). Some icons and wall paintings in the chapel are inscribed in Slavonic. The several languages used in the icons reflect the linguistic practices of the local Orthodox community and visitors to the chapel.

Ouspensky was asked to paint the walls of this church next, which had been prepared according to his specifications for live fresco. His age and declining health, however, prevented him from fresco painting, which requires great physical stamina. He assigned one of his pupils to continue that work, and at the writing of this book, it remains in progress. Another student (a monk of

Plate 43 Exterior of the Church

Mount Athos) is finishing the uncompleted icon screen (the lower range: Christ, Virgin with Child; the Deacon's Doors [north and south doors] with the Holy Archangels Michael and Gabriel; and the Royal Doors).

SS Guria and Shamuna lived in Edessa during the reign of Diocletian, and were beheaded for confessing Christ in AD 288. St Habib the Deacon was burned alive in AD 316, and was buried with the other two saints. They are honored by the Church as martyrs and confessors. Sharing the same burial place and feast day, they are portrayed together in their icons.

Plate 44 SAINTS GURIA, SHAMUNA
AND HABIB THE DEACON
Private collection of S. and
C. Aslanov, 1960
Egg tempera on gessoed wood

Plate 45 Detail:
SAINTS GURIA, SHAMUNA AND
HABIB THE DEACON (Plate 44)

Plate 46 FOLDING TRIPTYCH WITH DEISIS AND PATRON SAINTS
29 cm x 18.1 cm
Private collection of N. and V. Lossky, 1985
Egg tempera on gessoed wood

This complex composition is a family icon, that is, an ensemble composed of the patron saints of the family for which the icon was painted, depicted around a central figure—in this case, the Deisis (Christ at center, with the Virgin and St John the Forerunner to the viewer's left and right respectively). Above the Deisis in a carved dome-shaped space is the depiction of the Holy Trinity—the three angels who appeared to Abraham and Sarah at the Oak of Mamre.[26] In the upper spaces of the side panels are the Prophets Elijah and Daniel (to the viewer's left and right respectively). To the right of St John the Forerunner stand the Archangel Michael and St Paul; to the left of the Virgin, the Archangel Gabriel and St Peter. In the bottom row, from left to right, are shown St Geneviève of Paris, St Romanos the Melodist,

St Michael of Tver, St Nicholas of Myra, St Veronica, St Andrew the Apostle, St Anna, St Vladimir, and St Valentina. The background color around each saint is a light, warm ivory. The figures are set within a carved raised border which has been left unpainted, the natural wood surface being both beautiful and practical, as the icon may be folded shut and easily transported. At their baptism, Orthodox Christians are given the name of a saint who becomes their patron saint and is remembered in daily prayer. For many Orthodox, it is their patron saint's feast day, rather than their own birthday, that is celebrated. Family icons form an entire category of iconography, and are usually set up in the place where the family gathers for prayer.

26 Genesis 18. See also the description of Plates 20 and 21 (pp. 32–33).

49

Plate 47 SAINT ANNA HOLDING THE VIRGIN
27.8 cm x 20.6 cm
Private collection of J.-C. and A. Larchet, 1980
Egg tempera on gessoed wood

St Anna was of the priestly tribe of Levi. She and her husband, St Joachim, were loosed from barrenness in their old age when the child Mary was born. They offered her to God in fulfillment of a vow and in thanksgiving for the miracle in their old age, by which the Mother of the Word herself came into the world. St Anna wears the traditional bright red robe, and holds the Mother of God in her arms. St Anna is celebrated three times during the year (July 25, September 9, and December 9), and she figures prominently in Orthodox iconography and veneration. Writing on the birth of the Virgin Mary, Vladimir Lossky said:

> In the person of St Anna—a woman freed from her sterility to bring into the world a Virgin who would give birth to God incarnate—it is our nature which ceased to be sterile in order to start bearing the fruits of grace.[27]

The icon on the page 51 (plate 48) depicts the Virgin, seated on a throne, surrounded by Old Testament prophets, her hands raised in intercession. It is called "The Praises of the Most Holy Virgin." She glances down and to her right, and is presented within a space defined by a wreath of flowering plants. Above her is Christ, depicted as a child with his hands raised in blessing, within a space defined by the same floral border. The prophets on the left (at the top) are Habakkuk and Jacob (with the ladder) ; under them, Aaron (with the priest's head covering, holding a flowering staff) and Moses; below them, King Solomon (the younger figure) and the Prophet King David (the older figure). On the right (at the top) are the Prophets Zachariah and Elijah; below them, Jeremiah (the younger figure) and Ezekiel; below them, Isaiah holding a burning coal, and Gideon holding a fleece. Kneeling below the Virgin is the Prophet Barlaam (a son of Jacob), who holds a star. The prophets hold open scrolls with texts from the Old Testament that the Church Fathers understood to contain prophetic images of the Virgin and of the Incarnation of God in particular. For example, the Prophet Jacob holds a ladder, and his text reads: "I beheld thee in a dream as a ladder reaching from the earth up to the heavenly city," referring to his prophetic dream recounted in Genesis 28:11–17. Barlaam holds a star, in reference to his foretelling of the coming of the Messiah: ". . . there shall come a Star out of Jacob, and a Scepter shall rise out of Israel . . ." (Numbers 24:17). Many of the references on the icon are mentioned in the text of the service in honor of the Virgin that is celebrated on the fifth Saturday of Great Lent, from which the icon takes its name.

27 See Leonid Ouspensky and Vladimir Lossky, *The Meaning of Icons* (Crestwood, NY: St Vladimir's Seminary Press, 1982), 146.

ПОХВАЛА ПРЕСТЫА БЦЫ

Plate 48 THE PRAISES OF THE MOST HOLY VIRGIN
31 cm x 25 cm
Private collection of M. Berge, 1954
Egg tempera on gessoed linden wood

In this remarkably beautiful icon on page 53, St John the Baptist is pictured against a background of light olive green with a golden underpainting. A brown cloak of coarse fur half covers his body. His hair and beard are unkempt—the usual manner of depicting desert-dwelling ascetics—which underlines the wilderness setting of his preaching: "I saw and bear record that this is the Son of God."[28] He gazes directly at the viewer and points with his right hand to the text that is the key to his role in the Christian gospel. The Forerunner is seen bearing witness to the Son in both the icon of the Theophany (plate 49, below) and in the icon of The Descent into Hell (plate 84).

Plate 49 THE BAPTISM OF CHRIST
25 cm x 16 cm
Church of Our Lady, Joy of All Who Sorrow and
St Geneviève of Paris, rue Saint-Victor, Paris, circa 1960
Egg tempera on gessoed wood

28 Mt 3:1; Mk 1:4; Lk 3:2.

Plate 50 SAINT JOHN THE BAPTIST
32 cm x 25.5 cm
Private collection of M. Mihalick, 1983
Egg tempera on gessoed wood

Plate 51 SAINT BASIL THE BLESSED, FOOL FOR CHRIST'S SAKE
Church of Our Lady, Joy of All Who Sorrow
and St Geneviève of Paris
Rue Saint-Victor, Paris
Egg tempera on gessoed wood

Plate 52 SAINT SERAPHIM OF SAROV
Private collection of M. Fortounatto
Egg tempera on gessoed wood

St Basil the Blessed, a fifteenth-century ascetic and Fool for Christ, lived in the public streets of Moscow, keeping silent prayer as if he lived in a desert hermitage. He went about in rags or even naked, and is usually shown thus in his icon. The naked body is represented here without sensuality or excessive attention to details. The saint stands in the state of restored human purity, praying before the Mother of God.

For much of his life, St Seraphim of Sarov lived in a solitary cell in a remote forest, passing long periods of time in prayer. On one occasion, he was attacked by robbers, and left almost dead, his chest and head badly crushed, and his body permanently bent. The painter has shown the physical deformity of the saint, without making it a focal point of the depiction. Quite the contrary, his infirmity is incorporated into the posture of his intense and heartfelt prayer.

Plate 53 SAINT TIKHON OF
ZADONSK
30 cm x 23.2 cm
Church of the Three Holy
Hierarchs, rue Petel,
Paris, 1965
Egg tempera on gessoed wood

St Tikhon (1724–1783) was a prolific writer of spiritual texts and served the Church as a bishop. He is depicted here in a monastic veil and hat (Orthodox bishops are chosen from the ranks of the monastics). St Tikhon had become a monk at the age of thirty-four but retired to a monastery in the midst of his episcopal career. He holds a bishop's staff in his left hand (staffs usually have an embroidered cloth tied at the top, with which the staff is held), his right hand raised in blessing. He wears the embroidered outer garment, or *mantiya,* associated with the episcopacy (a simpler *mantiya* is worn by monks), and an oval pendant around his neck, another episcopal prerogative, called a *Panagia* ("All-Holy One" =Greek, a liturgical term for the Virgin Mary who is usually depicted on these episcopal pendants). This *Panagia* is painted with a small icon of the Virgin of the Sign (plate 23, p. 35). St Tikhon directs an austere gaze at the viewer. He was canonized in 1861, and his feast day is celebrated on August 13.[29]

29 For a detailed biography, see Nadejda Gorodetzky, *St Tikhon of Zadonsk, Inspirer of Dostoevsky* (Crestwood, NY: St Vladimir's Seminary Press, 1976).

Plate 54 SAINT JOHN CHRYSOSTOM
25.5 cm x 19.4 cm
Private collection of J.-C. and A. Larchet, 1985
Egg tempera on gessoed wood

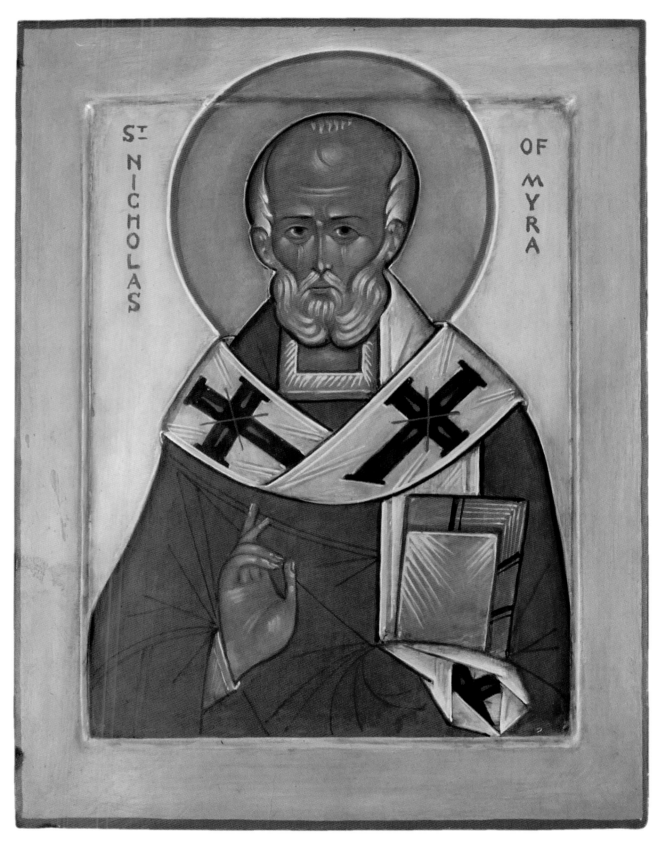

Plate 55 SAINT NICHOLAS OF MYRA
32 cm x 25.5 cm
Private collection of M. Mihalick. 1980
Egg tempera on gessoed wood

Plates 56 and 57
Detail: Saint Geneviève of Paris with Scenes from Her Life (Plate 59)

Plate 56 Saint Geneviève heals a blind man

Plate 57 Saint Geneviève casts out a demon

Plate 58 Saint Geneviève
22 cm x 13 cm
Private collection of S. and C. Aslanov, 1966
Metal repoussé (pressed silver-plated copper, mounted on a wooden support)

St Geneviève (AD 423–512) lived a life of extraordinary personal asceticism and charity to the people of Paris, and she was early designated its patron saint.[30] She is depicted in a deep green robe with a white veil, against a bright red background. In the border around the figure of the saint are, at top center, the Deisis with Christ, the Virgin (left) and St John the Forerunner (right). Continuing (right) from the Forerunner are Archangel Gabriel, St Paul, and St Irenaeus of Lyon, and (left) from the Virgin are Archangel Michael, St Peter, and St Dionysios. The scenes from St Geneviève's life are read from left to right in parallel across the panel: (1) St Germain of Auxerre blesses St Geneviève (2) St Geneviève takes the veil, that is to say, she embraces the monastic life (3) St Geneviève blesses the construction of the basilica of St Dionysios (4) St Geneviève heals a young girl (5) St Geneviève heals a blind man (6) St Geneviève casts out a demon (7) St Geneviève brings bread to Paris, and (8) the death of St Geneviève. The *troparion* (hymn) sung to her is inscribed in French across the bottom border of the icon. Her feast day is observed on January 3, the day of her death.

30 For her *Life*, see Hieromonk Makarios of Simonos Petra, *The Synaxarion*, vol. 3 (Ormylia: Holy Convent of the Annunciation of of Our Lady, 1999).

Plate 59 SAINT GENEVIÈVE OF PARIS WITH SCENES FROM HER LIFE
50 cm x 39.2 cm
Church of Our Lady, Joy of All Who Sorrow and St Geneviève of Paris, rue Saint-Victor, Paris, 1984
Egg tempera on gessoed wood

Plate 60 SAINT SILOUAN THE ATHONITE
17 cm x 14 cm
Private collection
Egg tempera on gessoed wood

Plate 61 SAINT SILOUAN THE ATHONITE
Photograph

St Silouan the Athonite is one of the most extraordinary saints of the twentieth century. He died at St Panteleimon's Monastery on Mount Athos in 1938 after a life of singular asceticism, personal humility, and simplicity. Gifted with rare ability as a spiritual struggler, his life is recounted in a detailed biography written by his best-known disciple, Archimandrite Sophrony (Sakharov) of Essex.[31] His feast day is September 11. Ouspensky painted several of the earliest known icons of St Silouan the Athonite.

In both icons shown here, the saint is depicted in monastic garb, with a light cassock under a black *rason*, and the traditional monastic veil and hat. His gaze is directed towards Christ, who appears in a mandorla blessing Silouan, whose right hand is raised in prayer. He holds an open scroll in his left hand with a text from his writings: "I pray to Thee, Merciful Lord, that all the peoples of the earth will know Thee by the Holy Spirit." The composition is classic and simple, giving the praying figure of the saint great power as we follow his gaze towards the Savior.

31 Archimandrite Sophrony (Sakharov), *Saint Silouan the Athonite,* trans. Rosemary Edmonds (Crestwood, NY: St Vladimir's Seminary Press, 1991.)

Plate 62 Saint Silouan the Athonite
Private collection
Egg tempera on gessoed wood

Plate 63
Detail:
SAINT NEKTARIOS
OF AEGINA
(Plate 64)

St Nektarios is the most renowned and popular of modern Greek saints. He was born in 1846 and died in 1920. He was canonized in 1961, and his feast day is observed on November 9. He was briefly Bishop of Pentapolis in Egypt at the end of the nineteenth century. Released from his episcopal duties in Egypt, he went to Greece where he was instrumental in rehabilitating a prominent school near Athens, the Rizarios School, which has produced generations of leaders of national importance. His relics on the island of Aegina are one of the most popular pilgrimage sites in the world. He is depicted here in his austere monastic, rather than episcopal, garb—black *rason,* veil, and *kamilavka*. He holds the Gospel in his reverently covered left hand, his right hand is raised in blessing. He looks directly at the viewer with a gaze that is at once meek and commanding. The border is painted a translucent sienna, and the interior background is a warm ivory. The composition is reduced to bare essentials, and achieves its powerful effect through the painter's control of a deliberately restrained range of sharply-defined contours and colors. Grace and strength combine on this panel with meekness and charity, characteristics well established in the saint's lifelong practice of strict asceticism and humble service to the Church.[32]

32 For this and other biographical details, see Dr Constantine Cavarnos, *St Nectarios of Aegina*, vol. 7 in the author's Modern Orthodox Saints series, (Belmont, MA: Institute for Byzantine and Modern Greek Studies, 1981).

ST NECTAIRE D'EGINE

Plate 64 Saint Nektarios of Aegina
30 cm x 22 cm
Church of Our Lady, Joy of All Who Sorrow and St Geneviève of Paris,
Rue Saint-Victor, Paris, circa 1960
Egg tempera on gessoed wood

Plate 65 Detail: SAINT SERGIUS OF RADONEZH (Plate 66)

Plate 66 SAINT SERGIUS OF RADONEZH
45.5 cm x 35.5 cm
St Gregory of Sinai Monastery,
Kelseyville, California, 1980
Egg tempera on gessoed wood

St Sergius of Radonezh (1313–1392), the most popular of all Russian saints, lived at a time of acute national crisis as the nation struggled to emerge from the demoralizing Tatar occupation, a struggle in which he played a central, constructive role.[33] St Sergius understood Russia's predicament during this period to be essentially a spiritual crisis, involving personal and national renewal through ascetical effort. He endowed the rebirth of Russia's national culture with religious depth, and gave monasticism a permanent and central place within that culture. St Sergius is depicted in monastic garb—dark brown *mantiya* over a light-colored cassock. The

schema, a sign of monastic standing, is worn over the saint's shoulders and is visible, hanging directly down over his chest, under his *mantiya* and belt. His left hand holds a teacher's scroll, his right hand is raised in blessing. He directs a gaze of intense inner peace and strength towards the viewer. The background is painted a light ivory, with a painted gold halo. The large areas of solid color and the simplicity of contour and line give the image great austerity and spiritual power, fully in keeping with the biography of this ascetic saint. The saint's name is inscribed in Slavonic. The saint's feast days are July 5 and September 25.

---

33 Pierre Kovalevsky, *Saint Sergius and Russian Spirituality* (Crestwood, NY: St Vladimir's Seminary Press, 1976), offers a good summary of St Sergius' life and significance.

Plate 67 THE NATIVITY OF CHRIST
28 cm x 22.3 cm
Church of Our Lady,
Joy of All Who Sorrow
and St Geneviève of Paris
Rue Saint-Victor, Paris, 1964
Egg tempera on gessoed wood

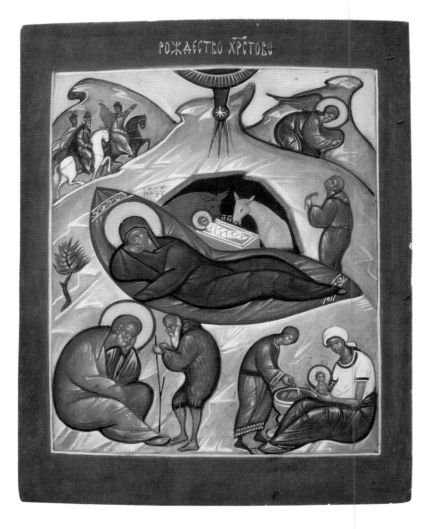

The Adoration of the Magi (plate 68) is a large wall composition that follows a format essentially unchanged from the earliest extant depiction of the subject in the Roman catacombs.[34] The Savior is depicted in gold garments seated on the lap of the Virgin Mary. He holds a teacher's scroll in his left hand, his right hand raised in blessing. The Virgin is seated on a gold throne, her feet supported on a footstool. Her right hand rests on her Son's shoulder, drawing our gaze toward him. The three Magi, or Wise Men, approach from our left in attitudes of reverent awe and worship. Clad in richly colored garments, they wear exotic, oriental head coverings and bear their gifts of gold, frankincense, and myrrh in hands that are covered in respect. The faithful, standing in the nave beneath this mural, see themselves as assembling behind the Magi to approach the God made flesh along with them:

Come O ye faithful, and let us behold where
    Christ is born.
Let us join the Magi, kings from the East, and
    follow the guiding star. . . .[35]

This mural, painted on the north wall of the Church of the Three Hierarchs in Paris, is strikingly similar to the ancient Roman fresco (plate 69) painted at the beginning of the third century in the Catacomb of Priscilla in Rome. Although the older fresco is very faded and worn, one can see that the iconography of the Adoration of the Magi has changed very little over the better part of two thousand years. The Adoration of the Magi has been incorporated into the icon of the Nativity of Christ, sometimes showing the Magi coming before the Virgin and Child on foot, as in our wall paintings, and sometimes seen approaching from afar, on horseback, still following the star, as seen in Ouspensky's panel icon pictured above (plate 67).

34 See Andre Grabar, *The Origins of Christian Iconography* (London: Routledge and Kegan Paul, 1969), 8.
35 Matins in the Orthodox liturgical cycle for the "Nativity According to the Flesh," first Sessional Hymn, Tone 4.

Plate 68 THE ADORATION OF THE MAGI
89 cm x 56 cm
Church of the Three Hierarchs, rue Petel, Paris, 1960
Egg tempera mural on lime plaster

Plate 69 THE ADORATION OF THE MAGI
Catacomb of Priscilla, Rome
Early third-century fresco

At the center of the icon (plate 71), the Holy Cross of the Savior is held aloft in the midst of a multitude by the Patriarch of Jerusalem, Macarius, who is bareheaded and clad in the *polystavrion* ("many crosses" =Greek) *phelonion*. He is supported left and right by two deacons, each in a long robe called a *sticharion*. The three-barred cross seen here is the most frequently shown cross design in Byzantine and Russian iconography. The three crossbars are simply explained: the upper bar stands for the inscription placed over the Cross at Pilate's order; the center bar for the extended arms; and the bottom, slanted bar holds the body's weight during the prolonged asphyxiation that resulted in the death of crucified victims. The ascending and descending angles of the foot bar often remind worshippers of the just, who stand to the right and ascend, and the damned, who remain on the left and descend.[36] These details can be observed in several of the crosses Ouspensky carved on wood, such as that shown in Plate 70. The icon of the Elevation of the Holy Cross commemorates the discovery of the true Cross by St Helen, the mother of the emperor, St Constantine the Great, in about the year AD 325, an event celebrated each year on the Orthodox church calendar on September 14. To the viewer's left, their hands extended in supplication, stand the Emperor Constantine and Empress Helen. They are clothed in pearl-studded crowns and imperial garments edged in

gold-highlighted scarlet. The background is composed of an architectural grouping representing Jerusalem. The Empress Helen, desiring to recover the True Cross, undertook a search in Jerusalem for the relic. It was found, miraculously confirmed to be the True Cross, and became one of the primary focuses of Christian pilgrimage and veneration. The composition is centered on the large Cross, towards which our attention is drawn by the eight figures surrounding it. The dark blue robe of the figure of the blind man and the red *maforion* of the woman to our right, balance the dark blue-and-red clad imperial figures to our left. The white vestments of the Patriarch and deacons, together with the facade of the church in the background, combine to provide a unified field of bright light that encompasses the Holy Cross. The outstretched arms of the Patriarch exalting the newly discovered Cross constitute a powerful gesture that visually reinforces the centrality of the Cross, as do the two figures supporting the Patriarch.

Plate 70 CARVED GRAVE CROSS
Grave of Father Sergius Bulgakov
Russian Cemetery, Sainte Geneviève-des-
Bois Cemetery, Paris, 1945–1946
Carved wood

36 Cf. a reference from the *Octoechos*, a book containing the cycle of liturgical services relating to the eight musical tones in the Orthodox Church, Monday Matins, Sessional Hymn, Tone 8.

ВОЗДВИЖЕНІЕ КРСТА ГДНА

Plate 71 THE EXALTATION OF THE CROSS OF THE LORD
30 cm x 23 cm
Church of the Three Holy Hierarchs, rue Petel Paris, circa 1950
Egg tempera on gessoed wood

Plate 72 THE RESURRECTION OF CHRIST
30 cm x 23.3 cm
Church of the Three Holy Hierarchs, rue Petel, Paris, circa 1950
Egg tempera on gessoed wood

Plate 73 SAINT MARY MAGDALENE
30 cm x 23.2 cm
Church of the Three Holy Hierarchs, rue Petel, Paris, circa 1965
Egg tempera on gessoed wood

The image of the myrrh-bearing women at the empty tomb is the most ancient representation of the Resurrection.[37] The oldest that has come down to us dates from the early third century.[38] In the icon shown in Plate 74, details of the scriptural account[39] are represented: the women approach, carrying spices for the anointing of the dead, and find an angel in shining white garments, sitting upon the stone, which has been rolled away, his right hand raised in blessing. The grave clothes lie in the empty tomb; the cloths that had wrapped Christ's head and those that had wrapped his body retain their shapes and lie separately from one another, a fact that struck St John the Beloved Disciple "who saw and believed."[40] The group of myrrh-bearing women is balanced by the larger vigorous figure of the archangel. The combined figures, facing the grave from both sides of the panel, powerfully focuses the viewer's attention on the empty tomb and the Resurrection. In spite of the greater complexity of this subject, the presentation remains one of simplicity of contour and presentation.

To this representation may be added a second episode on the same panel: Christ appearing to St Mary Magdalene, as shown in the icon above, in Plate 72. St Mary looks up from the empty tomb and, seeing Christ, supposes him to be the gardener. St Mary Magdalene, also shown in the icon at in Plate 73, is called "the Apostle to the Apostles."[41] The title comes from the accounts in the Gospels where St Mary is sent to the apostles by Christ himself and by the angel at the empty tomb, to announce the Resurrection.

37 Cf. *The Origins of Christian Iconography,* by Andre Grabar (London: Routledge and Kegan Paul, 1969), 123–124.

38 See p. 6, n. 2.

39 Mt 28; Mk 16; Lk 24; Jn 20.

40 Jn 20: 1–8.

41 For details of her life, cf. "Marie Madeleine," in *The Synaxarion,* by Hieromonk Makarios of Simonos Petra, Tome 5 (Thessalonica: Editions To Perivoli tis Panaghias, 1996), 196–201.

Plate 74 THE RESURRECTION OF CHRIST
24 cm x 19 cm
Private collection of J. Forstmann
Egg tempera on gessoed wood

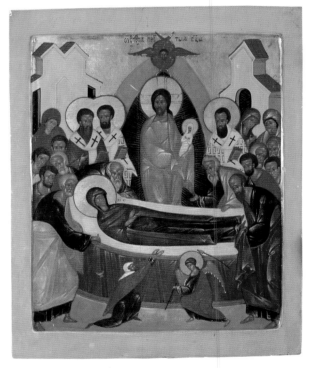

Plates 75–78 FESTAL ICONS
31 cm x 24 cm (approx.), Church of the Three Holy Hierarchs, rue Petel, Paris, circa 1950
Egg tempera on gessoed wood
Plate 75: THE PRESENTATION OF THE VIRGIN MARY IN THE TEMPLE; Plate 76: THE PRESENTATION OF CHRIST IN THE TEMPLE (from top left)
Plate 77: THE ASCENSION OF CHRIST; Plate 78: THE DORMITION OF THE VIRGIN MARY (from bottom left)

The five icons on this page and on page 73 are part of the full set of festal icons of the Church of the Three Holy Hierarchs in Paris, which were painted over the course of several years. They are (above, clockwise from the top left) the Presentation of the Virgin in the Temple, the Presentation of Christ in the Temple, the Dormition of the Virgin, and the Ascension of Christ. On the facing page is the icon of Pentecost.

Plate 79 PENTECOST
31 cm x 24 cm (approx.)
Church of the Three Holy Hierarchs, rue Petel, Paris, circa 1950
Egg tempera on gessoed wood

Plate 80 THE TRANSFIGURATION
30 cm x 23 cm
Church of the Three Holy Hierarchs, rue Petel,
Paris , circa 1950
Egg tempera on gessoed wood

Thou wast transfigured upon the mountain,
and Thy disciples beheld Thy glory, O Christ
    our God,
as far as they were able so to do:
that when they saw Thee crucified,
they might know that Thy suffering was
    voluntary,
and might proclaim unto the world
that Thou art truly the Brightness of the
    Father.
Kontakion for the feast of the Transfiguration

The Orthodox Church celebrates the feast of the Transfiguration on August 6, commemorating the event noted in Matthew 17, Mark 9:2, Luke 9:29, John 1:14, and 2 Peter 1:16. Christ took the Apostles Peter, James, and John up to a high mountain—traditionally Mount Tabor—where the Prophets Moses and Elijah appeared conversing with him, while his own appearance was transfigured with an unearthly brightness.

Liturgical texts for the feast emphasize the immediacy and the intensity of the apostles' awareness of Jesus' divinity on the mountain, and the theme of the bright, unearthly light, or "the light of Tabor," plays an important role in that strain of mysticism known as the hesychast movement. The icons pictured show the unusual character of the event—the stately calm of Christ standing transfigured before us, the reverence of the two Old Testament prophets, and the unusual situation of the apostles, who literally tumble about, shielding their eyes while participating in the startling event "as far as they were able." The light of the Godhead shining from Christ, illumining those around him, and the world beneath his feet are set before the congregation in both the icon and in the hymns sung on the feast itself:

Today on Tabor in the manifestation of Thy
    Light, O Word,
Thou unaltered Light from the Light of the
    unbegotten Father,

we have seen the Father as Light and the Spirit as
    Light,
guiding with light the whole creation.
Exapostilarion, Matins for the feast of the
    Transfiguration

Writing on hesychasm and humanism Ouspensky says of this light:

The Taboric light is one of the modes of God's manifestation or revelation in the world; it is a presence of the uncreated within the created order, a presence that is not allegorical but actually revealed and contemplated by the saints, and ineffable beauty. Unknowable in his nature, God thus communicates himself to man through his operations, deifying man's entire being and making him God-like. "And when the saints contemplate this divine light within themselves they behold the garment of their deification" (St Gregory Palamas, *Triad* 1.5). This divine grace is not merely an object of faith; it is also an object of concrete, living experience.[42]

42 Ouspensky, *Theology of the Icon*, 239.

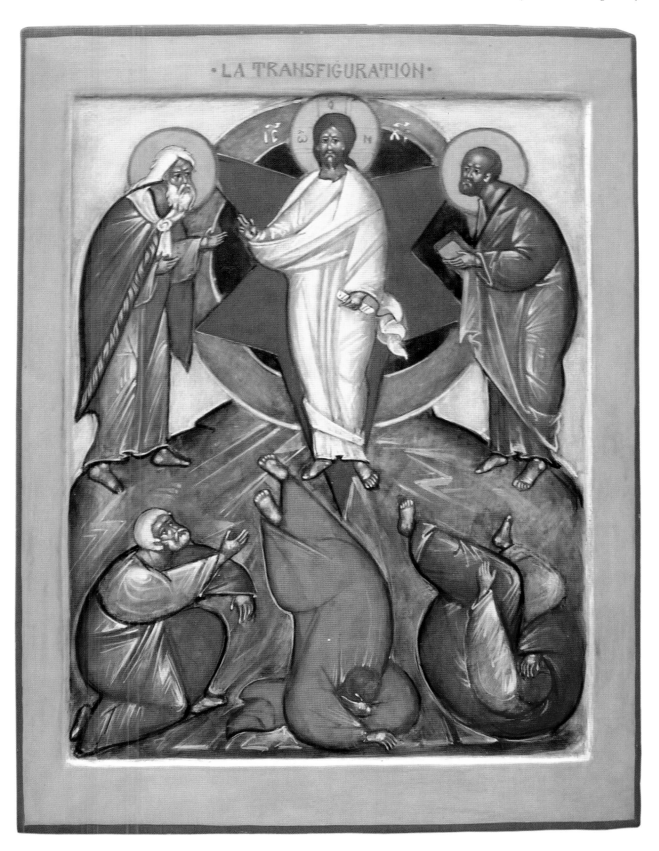

·LA TRANSFIGURATION·

Plate 81 THE TRANSFIGURATION
11.5 cm x 8.7 cm
Private collection J. Minet, 1965
Egg tempera on gessoed wood

Plate 82 HAND BLESSING CROSS
Front view
Church of Our Lady, Joy of All Who Sorrow and
St Geneviève of Paris
Rue Saint-Victor, Paris, circa 1950
Bronze metal repoussé , mounted on a wooden core

Plate 83 HAND BLESSING CROSS
Back view
Church of Our Lady, Joy of All Who Sorrow and
St Geneviève of Paris
Rue Saint-Victor, Paris, circa 1950
Bronze metal repoussé, mounted on a wooden core

In the icon pictured in Plate 84, Christ stands at the center of a circular mandorla, gold rays emanating from his body. He leans to his left, extending his right hand to Adam who emerges from a sarcophagus in an attitude of supplication. To Christ's right, Eve has already been raised and kneels in prayer. To the left and right, figures from the Old and New Testaments bear witness to the raising of Adam and Eve from the dead. Beneath Christ's feet, hell appears as a black pit of unfathomable depth, and two crossed doors signal the destruction of the gates of hell. Behind the mandorla, a landscape of barren rock forms the entrance to the cave of hell. An edge of Christ's robe flies up behind his left shoulder, indicating dynamic movement and contrasting with the serenity of

his expression. His stance is powerful as he pulls Adam and Eve out of death with a forceful gesture. The presence of so many figures results in a compositional complexity balanced by the painter's characteristically restrained approach to color, contour, and layout.

A silver-plated copper border in repoussé (one of the many media used by Ouspensky) has been worked in a continuous pattern of twining leaves and vines, with cruciform flowerettes at each corner, adding to the overall impression of elegance and richness appropriate to this culminating vision of Christian faith. The technique of metal repoussé, also used to produce the hand-blessing cross above, is described on the page 78.

Plate 84 DESCENT INTO HELL
28 cm x 24.1 cm
Church of Our Lady, Joy of All Who Sorrow
and St Geneviève of Paris, rue Saint-Victor Paris, circa 1966
Icon: egg tempera on gessoed wood
Border: silver-plated copper metal repoussé

Plate 85 METAL GOSPEL COVER
Front view: 34.3 cm x 24.3 cm
Church of Our Lady, Joy of All Who Sorrow and St Geneviève of Paris
Rue Saint-Victor, Paris, circa 1975
Silver-plated copper repoussé

The medium used for an icon is selected with regard to its placement and function. The two icons on these facing pages make up the front and reverse covers of a Gospel book used in liturgical services. Because the article is handled and moved about during the service, the medium has to be both durable and beautiful. In metal repoussé, a medium often used by Ouspensky, the image is made by inscribing (actually pressing) the thin sheet of metal, first on the front, then on the reverse, back and forth until the icon is completed in a low relief that pres-

ents the image in light and shadow instead of colors.

On the front cover of the Gospel book, Christ the Pantokrator is seated on a throne, centered in a large oval mandorla. He holds a Gospel in his left hand, resting on his knee; his right hand is raised in blessing. Around the border of the mandorla are the symbols of the four Evangelists (plates 2 and 3, pp. 18–19). The space around the figures is filled with a pebbled surface, which contrasts with the relatively smooth surface of the background within the mandorla. The overall effect is one of great simplicity,

Plate 86 METAL GOSPEL COVER
Back view: 34.3 cm x 24.3 cm
Church of Our Lady, Joy of All Who Sorrow and St Geneviève of Paris
Rue Saint-Victor, Paris, circa 1975
Silver-plated copper repoussé

giving maximum attention to the central seated figure of Christ. During the office of Matins, the priest, after the Gospel reading, processes to the center of the church with the Gospel held up for all to see, as the congregation sings, "Having beheld the Resurrection of Christ, let us worship the Lord Jesus . . ." Again, at the Eucharistic Liturgy, the Gospel is carried aloft in procession through the congregation in preparation for its proclamation. The icon completes the liturgical action: it is a visualization of the theological meaning of the liturgical act.

On the reverse of the Gospel cover is the Crucifixion. At the center, in a beautifully curving mandorla, are the crucified Christ with the Virgin Mary, St John the Beloved Disciple, and two angels at the top. The Cross has three bars (see also plate 70, p. 68). The walls of Jerusalem appear in the background and Adam's skull is depicted beneath the Cross, since Golgotha, the site of the crucifixion, is the traditional burial site of Adam. In the four corners are the Evangelists (clockwise from upper right) Matthew, Mark, Luke, and John.

Plate 87 CARVED KIOT FRAME
153 cm x 85 cm
Church of the Three Holy Hierarchs, rue Petel, Paris, circa 1950
Carved walnut

Plate 88 Detail: CARVED KIOT FRAME (Plate 87)
Right side: cherubim and ornamental animal figures

Plate 89 Detail: CARVED KIOT FRAME
(Plate 87)
St John Of Damascus

Plate 90 Detail: CARVED KIOT FRAME (Plate 87)
Front piece: 34 cm x 85 cm

Plate 91 Detail: CARVED KIOT FRAME (Plate 87)
Our Lady, Joy of All Who Sorrow

Ouspensky was commissioned to carve the kiot, or shrine, built to hold this eighteenth-century Russian icon of the Virgin and Child,[43] for the nave of the Russian Orthodox Church of the Three Holy Hierarchs in Paris. The carved panel of the "Our Lady, Joy of All Who Sorrow" runs across the top of the framework. The icon is inspired by the hymn of the same name, which is sung at the service of Compline. The Virgin stands in the midst of a large throng, inclined to the entreaties of the afflicted who approach her from left and right in attitudes of supplication and veneration. At the far right is a ship in peril at sea, filled with suppliants. In the two curved panels just below this top panel are St John of Damascus (to the viewer's left, detail shown on p. 80) and St Romanos the Melodist (to the viewer's right). Both saints composed often-sung hymns of praise to the Virgin, the first lines of which are shown on the scrolls they hold. On the sides of the frame are cherubim and ornamental motifs of animals and vines.

---

43 In 1983, Ouspensky was commissioned to restore the damaged icon itself, which had been discovered in an antique store and bought by the congregation for the then-enormous sum of 25,000 francs.

Plate 92 HAND BLESSING CROSS
29.4 cm x 15.9 cm
St Gregory of Sinai Monastery
Kelseyville, California, 1980
Carved walnut

Plate 93 BAPTISMAL CROSS
Private collection of C. Aslanov, 1964
Carved walnut

The grave cross shown in Plate 94 was carved for the Russian theologian Vladimir Lossky, who died in 1958. Lossky was Ouspensky's close friend, and was associated with him in the St Photios Brotherhood, a group of Orthodox intellectuals and artists working in Paris from the 1930s through the 1970s.[44] Lossky, author of the celebrated *Mystical Theology of the Eastern Church* and a renowned patristics scholar, collaborated with Ouspensky in writing *The Meaning of Icons*. Christ is depicted on this grave cross in repose after death, hanging from a traditional three-barred Cross. The three roundels contain: at the top, the myrrh-bearing women at the tomb with the angel; to the viewer's left, the Virgin Mary; and to the viewer's right, St Mary Magdalene.

44 See "A Short Biography," pp. 11–13.

Plate 98 Detail: CARVED CROSS
FOR A PANAKHIDA TABLE
(Plate 99)
50.8 cm x 35.5 cm
Church of the Three Hierarchs,
Rue Petel, Paris
Carved walnut

Plate 99 PANAKHIDA TABLE WITH
CARVED CROSS

ened, and the veil of the temple was rent in the midst."[45] Two angels are shown above with their hands covered in awe and reverence. The top part of the panel shows the All-Holy Trinity (plates 20 and 21, pp. 32–33). Beneath the cross is the skull of Adam, the First-created Man, for whom Christ died, that he might call him back to life. The wall of Jerusalem is seen in the slanted bar, and the spear and the rod with the sponge of vinegar stand on either side of the Savior.

The texts carved onto the cross grant insight to the meaning of the Crucifixion. Above the hands of Christ is written "Jesus Christ," while below his feet is the word "victorious." Above his head are the initials of Pilate's inscription, "Jesus Christ King of the Jews," and on either side of the halo are the words "The King of Glory." Below the arms of the Savior can be seen an Orthodox hymn carved in Slavonic: "We venerate Thy Cross, O Master, and Thy holy Resurrection we glorify."

45 Lk 23:44–45.

Plate 100 CHRIST PANTOKRATOR
60 cm x 50 cm
St Gregory of Sinai Monastery, Kelseyville, California, 1975
Carved walnut

Plate 101 Detail: CHRIST PANTOKRATOR (Plate 100)

Plate 102 Detail: CHRIST PANTOKRATOR (Plate 103)

Plate 103 CHRIST PANTOKRATOR
60 cm x 50 cm
St Gregory of Sinai Monastery
Kelseyville, California, 1975
Egg tempera on carved, gessoed walnut

This icon was originally done as a large, unpainted, carved walnut panel. Later Ouspensky gessoed and painted it—an effective combination of media seldom used for such icons. A rare photograph of this carved panel in its original unpainted state is presented in Plate 101. Christ is depicted seated in a central mandorla, his feet on a footstool. He holds a closed Gospel in his left hand, his right hand raised in blessing. He is clad in a dark wine-red robe, with a contrasting *clavus* over his right shoulder, and a deep blue himation over his robe. The border of the mandorla consists of a carved rope-pattern painted a light yellow ochre. The background of

the mandorla is a light, mottled green, and the area behind the lower half of Christ is a golden yellow ochre. Around the mandorla are the symbols of the four Evangelists (see plate 3, p. 19), as described in the Book of Revelation. They are painted in a red that is slightly lighter than that of the background itself, in order to be easily seen from a distance. The border of this icon is a deep earth green. The inscriptions for Christ are in Greek, while those of the Evangelists are in Latin. The iconographic content of this icon is identical with those of Plates 19 and 85, but in each icon a different medium is employed.

Plate 104
Detail: Carved Border
(Plate 105)

Plate 105 Double-Sided Processional Icon with Carved Frame
Front view: Our Lady of Georgia
Icon: 32.7 cm x 24 cm
Church of the Three Holy Hierarchs, rue Petel, Paris, circa 1960
Egg tempera on gessoed wood, with carved walnut frame and pole

Plate 106 DOUBLE-SIDED PROCESSIONAL ICON WITH CARVED FRAME
Back view: The Three Holy Hierarchs
Icon: 32.7 cm x 24 cm
Church of the Three Holy Hierarchs, rue Petel, Paris, circa 1960
Egg tempera on gessoed wood, with carved walnut frame and pole

Plates 107, 108, and 109 (from the top)
SAINT GREGORY THE THEOLOGIAN
SAINT JOHN CHRYSOSTOM
SAINT BASIL THE GREAT
30 cm x 23 cm
Church of the Three Holy Hierarchs, rue Petel, Paris, circa 1960
Egg tempera on gessoed wood

This double-sided icon has, on the front, Our Lady of Georgia, as this composition was known in Russia, and on the back, the Three Hierarchs: St Gregory the Theologian, St John Chrysostom, and St Basil the Great. These three Doctors of the Church share a common festal celebration on January 30, the feast to which this particular parish is dedicated. Ouspensky made and carved the frame, mounting the completed ensemble on a pole, so that the icon can be carried aloft in procession; at other times, it stands behind the altar table in a small holder made for it. The three bishops are shown in *polystavrion* ("many crosses"=Greek) *phelonia* (outer robes). To the right of the icon can be seen the same three bishops on three separate panels. Although celebrated together, each saint has also his own feast day (St Gregory, January 25; St John, November 1; and St Basil, January 1).

Plate 110 THE HOLY FACE
12 cm x 12 cm (approx.)
Wedding Icon, circa 1956
Carved stone

Ouspensky carved this monumental face of Christ in stone. It is the only known example of his use of this medium, which has been used by the Church since the earliest times.[46] The carving is simple and noble, the gently curving parallel lines of the hair and beard fram-ing the face, making good use of the solidity of the stone. It was commissioned to be a "Wedding Icon," that is, it was presented to a newly married couple at their wedding service.

46 We note the existence of many early Christian sarcophagi dating from the third century. Cf. "Sarcophagi, Early Christian," by M. Sotomayor, with bibliography, in *Encyclopedia of the Early Church,* volume II, ed. A. Di Bernardino (Oxford University Press, 1992).

Plate 111 SAINT AMVROSI OF OPTINA
18 cm x 13.5 cm
Private collection of Mme L. Ouspensky, 1986
Egg tempera on wood

This small icon of St Amvrosi of Optina was one of the last icons Ouspensky completed before his death in 1987. (There remained several unfinished icons, as he had been painting right up to the end of his life.) It shows the great teacher of ascetic prayer and Elder of Optina Monastery blessing with his right hand and in the other holding his prayer rope (Russian=*chotki*; Greek=*kombouskini*), a rope of knots used in the practice of the Jesus Prayer: "Lord Jesus Christ, Son God, have mercy on me a sinner."

Epilogue: Remembering Ouspensky

Leonid Alexandrovich Ouspensky was already 79 years old when I met him in 1981. I was to work under his direction for several months of each year until he died in December 1987.

I was among the last of a long line of pupils to come to the small flat he shared with his wife, Lydia Alexandrevna Ouspensky, at 39, rue Breguet to study with the master. I had a rudimentary beginning in iconography in the United States, studying with other icon painters and students of iconography.

Like many others, I first encountered Leonid Alexandrovich in his books, notably *The Meaning of Icons* and *The Theology of the Icon*. In the summer of 1981, the rector of my parish in Boston arranged for me to meet Ouspensky, to ask him to critique some of the work I had undertaken as of that date. We knew that he had retired from active teaching, and was accepting no new pupils, so our expectations were restrained. He replied to our request with an invitation to have dinner with him and his wife when I came to Paris.

I arrived in Paris in the fall of 1981, carrying photographs of some of my work, and many questions that had arisen during the preceding two years of struggling to learn the art of painting icons. I had no fixed return date, hoping that Ouspensky might be able to see me more than once. I telephoned him upon arrival, and Lydia Alexandrevna invited me to dinner the following evening at 5 p.m. As it happened, with jet lag and nervousness I lost my way the next evening and arrived three hours late for dinner. The Ouspensky's covered my embarrassment with a gracious and solicitous greeting, and insisted on feeding me before I began to speak with Leonid Alexandrovich about my work.

"Now then, what are your questions?" he asked when I was done. I was unprepared for so direct and immediate a beginning, and my mind, which had been full of questions, went blank. Then, put at ease by the simplicity of his words, we began to speak about icon painting, both its technical problems and its theoretical questions, that is, about the meaning of icons and their theological foundation.

As the evening progressed, it became clear that the technical questions—about paint, about egg tempera, about panel preparation and varnishing—that I had regarded as the most pressing, were easily and quickly answered, and we did not spend much time discussing them. Instead, the theology, the art, the meaning of the icon became the main topic of conversation. How are icons designed? Are old icons copied? How does one determine what is and what is not painted in an icon? How is one to understand the different styles observed in ancient and in contemporary icons? How is the creative ability of the painter used with regard to the need to paint something traditional? The evening's conversation opened up a new way of thinking about the icon, and a new way of approaching the problems inherent in painting an icon.

As he spoke to me about iconography, Leonid Alexandrovich illustrated the points he was making by referring to pictures in the books on iconography that lined the walls of his flat. On the mantle of the fireplace were several wood panels, leaning face to the wall. They were some of his own icons in various stages of completion and he used them, too, to illustrate certain points he was making. I became interested in these icons in particular. They were not copies of existing icons; at the same time, they were completely familiar. They emerged out of traditional patterns, without being copies of particular examples of the patterns. In the coming days, I would have chances to see many more of his icons in churches around Paris and in private homes where I was a guest. Always, there was a compelling combination of creativity and strict faithfulness to a traditional pattern.

Leonid Alexandrovich examined the photos of my work of the preceding two years closely. He noticed immediately that I was in the habit of tracing my icons from books, then transferring my tracing to a prepared panel, and painting the icon from there. He always noticed the difference between an icon based on a tracing and an icon painted from the underlying drawing by the painter or student himself. Here I received my first instruction: he told me that if I wanted to paint real icons, I would have to train to do my own drawing, having first studied good existing examples. Close observation and study of old icons had to be followed up with my own work. He told me that the painter has to understand the whole icon: its details, proportions, colors, but also the content, the meaning—everything, from within the received Tradition of the Church. Ouspensky wrote, in *The Meaning of Icons*:

> Therefore, the Church has repeatedly emphasized the necessity of following the Tradition, either through rulings of Councils, or through the voice of its dignitaries, and enjoined that icons should be painted "as the ancient holy iconographers painted them." "Portray in colors according to the Tradition," says St Simeon of Thessalonica, "this is painting as true as what is written in books, and the grace of God rests on it, for what is portrayed is holy." [The creation of an icon] has the character of catholic, not personal, creation. The iconographer transmits not his own "idea" but "a description of what is contemplated," which is factual knowledge . . . The usual "I see it like that," "I understand it this way," is entirely excluded in this case. The iconographer works not for himself, not for his own glory, but for the glory of God.[47]

Yet, immersion in the teaching of the Church about the holy icons and their meaning is just what gives the iconographer freedom: the artistic freedom to paint according to the holy faith. Again, from *The Meaning of Icons*:

> Iconography therefore is not copying. It is far from being impersonal, for to follow Tradition never shackles the creative powers of the iconographer, whose individuality expresses itself in the composition as well as in color and line. (. . .) The absence of identical icons has been noted long ago. Indeed, among icons on the same subject, although they are sometimes remarkably alike, we never find two identical icons (except in cases of deliberate copying in more modern times). Icons are not *copied*, but are *painted from*, which means their free creative transposition.[48]

This was the continuing paradox in Leonid Alexandrovich's teaching: in his school, there would be no exact reproductions of old icons, but there would always be vigorous study of the icon by constant, daily drawing from the ancient icons, which are themselves the guides and models for the iconographer.

Instead of tracing, there would be real drawing. Freedom would come from practice, familiarity with the old icons, and a growing understanding of the teaching of the Church, while living the life of the Church. By not reproducing other icons, there seemed to be an even greater need to understand the iconographic canon, and to study the icon in the light of scriptural reading, liturgical prayer, and patristic teaching. Leonid Alexandrovich never saw the icon as anything other than the art of the Church itself:

> Therefore, one can neither understand nor explain sacred art outside the Church and its life. Such an explanation would always be partial and incomplete. In relation to sacred art itself, it would be false.[49]

I asked what tools he used in his drawing, perhaps compasses or rulers? He was silent a moment, then held up his hand and said, "The hand. The hand is the best tool." As a rule, he did not use rulers, compasses, or any other measuring instrument to draw his icons on the panel. He drew freehand. As a result of this discipline, he was very sure-handed, and drew and painted the lines on his icons with an accuracy, freedom, and intensity rarely found in modern icon painters. One can see in the plates found in this book that the haloes are not drawn with a compass, but by hand. They are not perfect circles, but they are well drawn and correct with regard to the figures and proportions in the given icon.

The conversation that first night went on until very late; it seemed that the more questions I asked, the more questions I had. Finally, Lydia Alexandrevna turned to me and said (as she was to say on many evenings thereafter), "And now, Mr. Doolan, I am afraid we must turn you out." I thanked my hosts, packed my things, and left—a little dazed but grateful to have met and spoken with the master. I thought later that night that my journey had already been wonderful. I was excited about the work ahead, even if I did sense in some measure that I knew less than I had before I visited Leonid Alexandrovich! I did not know if I would see the Ouspenskys again, as nothing about a return visit had been mentioned, although I had mentioned that I had no fixed date of return to the United States. They had been quiet when I told them that. Lydia Alexandrevna phoned me

47 Ouspensky, *The Meaning of Icons*, 42.

48 Ibid., 43.

49 Ouspensky, *Theology of the Icon* Vol. 1, 8.

the next morning to say, "Come to the class at rue Petel on Saturday afternoon, and bring a pencil and paper." With that, I became a pupil of Leonid Ouspensky.

Ouspensky had taught a course of iconography on Saturday afternoons on the rue Petel for thirty years by the time I joined it. There were about twenty students when I arrived for my first class, of all ages and levels of study. In age, the class ranged from about 14 years to more than 60 years. The classroom was set up each week by Natalia Magdanovich, Ouspensky's able teaching assistant, a remarkable woman. She spoke a number of languages and translated for foreign students. There were several tables and a few students sat at each one. As they arrived, the students took out their materials and began to work. When Leonid Alexandrovich arrived at the class, it was always in his quiet, humble manner; but the atmosphere in the room changed noticeably. The students continued to paint or draw, but everyone would greet the master one by one with respect and then resume his work. On most days Ouspensky would go from pupil to pupil, looking at the work, offering criticism, instructing, demonstrating. Often several students trailed behind him to hear the advice he gave. This talk would sometimes develop into a lecture given to the entire class. As the students were at differing levels of achievement, from beginner to working iconographer, one heard instructions at all levels. One was expected to work in the class, so there was a rather limited opportunity to stop working and follow the master from table to table. But the room was small enough so that whatever instruction was given could be heard by everyone. Although some classes had a specific demonstration of technique scheduled, most of the time the course was run in an informal, "open" manner, with the instruction prompted as a response to a specific, individual drawing or painting. In that first class, by the time he got to my table, I was already drawing from a reproduction of an ancient icon, and he told me that he would see me later in the week at his studio; so I didn't receive any more instruction other than to be told to draw as much as I could every day.

I spent the following days in the church on rue Petel and in the Church of Our Lady, Joy of All Who Sorrow and St Geneviève on rue Saint-Victor, drawing and studying the icons of Ouspensky and those of the well-known Russian monk, Gregory Krug, and also from several old icons found in those churches. Later the next week, in Ouspensky's flat and in the very first hours of painting instruction, he began to talk about composition and application of colors. He concluded with an observation that took me by surprise: "There are no rules."

I thought I had misunderstood him, because we had been discussing the rules extensively, that is, the icono-graphic canon and its Tradition. It seemed to me that a study of the rules was something that one would spend one's life pursuing. But I had not understood to what his surprising remark referred. He was referring not to the content of the icon, but to the art of painting the icon. He did not use an approach that required—or even allowed—the same repetitive process, using the same premixed colors for each icon. Instead, he saw each icon on its own terms, to be painted from, and within, the Tradition—all the time remaining an authentically creative act. He told me that in the twentieth century, icons were usually painted in one of two extreme manners: either as a mechanical reproduction of an existing icon, or as a self-indulgent "original" artistic fantasy.

The Tradition of the Church is neither of these two extremes, he observed, but is creativity within the ecclesial Tradition. This explains why different people could regard his own work in such different ways. Some regarded him as excessively conservative, inflexible in matters of the icon's content. Others found his work modern and individualistic, because he did not copy, brush stroke for brush stroke, an ancient Russian or Byzantine icon. I believe that the examples of icons found in this book illustrate his understanding of faithfulness to Tradition, while employing his own creative gifts. For Ouspensky, these things were not opposed to each other; they were two indispensable components of traditional Orthodox icon painting. His own iconography appears to be executed in a very ancient style, and yet it is easy to identify his work as that of a gifted and sophisticated twentieth-century painter.

He often said, "The old icons are the best teachers" and, as Lydia Alexandrevna points out in her brief biography of her husband in this book, Ouspensky's teachers were the old icons to be found in France at that time. He required his students to encounter ancient icons face to face, *in situ*, and he was always interested in hearing about what his students saw, particularly when they were able to study icons that he had not been able to see himself. "You have to look at the old icons with six eyes!" he told me, as I set out one day to see some ancient icons in the Louvre. When I spent eighteen months in Greece in 1983–84, I visited him a number of times, and he wanted to hear about every church, every fresco, and every icon that I had seen. He would press for details.

Years later Lydia Alexandrevna told me that a group of people making a film approached Leonid Alexandrovich, asking if they could film him painting an icon. He found the idea extremely odd, and turned them out saying, "What next? You'll want to film me *praying*!" For Ouspensky, the bond between the icon and prayer was self-evident, primary, essential. And this was especially the case with *liturgical* prayer. He felt this keenly. Once,

97

years before, when he was beginning to paint icons, he was in the Church of the Three Hierarchs, and as the choir chanted, listening to the hymnography, he saw the connection between liturgical art and liturgical music, the church's iconography and the church's hymnology. They are interdependent; they imply and complete one another. He taught: "The icon completes the Liturgy."[50]

Ouspensky also had a great love and appreciation for the materials of the icon. He worked in different media, as this book illustrates—egg tempera for portable icons and wall paintings, carved wood, metal repoussé, and carved stone. He selected his materials very carefully and was able to fully appreciate their individual qualities. His egg tempera technique was as simple as it was classical. He rejected oil paint, a medium he knew well from his time as an art student and later as a secular artist, as inappropriate for iconography.[51] He mixed the pure pigments with a medium made of egg yolk, water, and vinegar, and applied these paints to a prepared gessoed wood panel.

For most of his professional life he made his own panels from linden or poplar wood, cutting the wood with a small handsaw, and carving out the face of the panel by hand in such a way as to leave a raised edge on all sides, using a chisel. He used the same simple tools to make the wood struts that he inserted across the back of the panel, to limit the warping of the wood over time.

He saturated the wood panel with hot gelatin glue, and then applied a piece of cotton to the panel, soaked in the same glue. When dry, the cloth surface of the panel was coated with several layers of gesso (Russian: *levkas*) made of hot glue and powdered marble or limestone, which he then sanded to a smooth finish, which in turn supported and held the layers of paint that would be applied.

Ouspensky began the drawing of the icon on the gessoed surface with a small amount of raw sienna pigment mixed with water. As this is not paint, but only a light tint, it would be easy to remove and change as the painting developed, improved, and underwent corrections as the painter searched for, and "found," the icon on the panel. Once this sienna sketch was sufficiently developed in outline, he switched to red ochre paint (a rusty red-brown) with egg medium added, and completed the drawing. He used red ochre for the final lines of the drawing because his egg tempera was always somewhat transparent. Red ochre, when covered over with other colors, is harmonious with them.

One day I saw an icon of the Annunciation in his studio, just begun. One could see two lightly sketched but indistinct figures, barely recognizable. It was hard to tell how large the sketchy, blurred figures would be in the finished icon. "I am still finding the forms," he told me. In other words, he had begun to draw the icon and although it may have been based on an earlier icon (or icons), this one would be a new icon, demanding all the creative abilities of the painter.

Ouspensky spent a great deal of time on this part of the process—often days, if not weeks, if something did not look right to him. He would lean it against the wall until he could work out the solution to the problem. Sometimes he scraped the image away altogether and began again. "You do your best, then a little better," Lydia Alexandrevna once said to me. This high standard was applied to icons great and small. I believe he saw no difference in an icon painted for an important location in a church and a small icon destined for an icon corner in a private home. He experienced the same struggle for both icons.

He would then apply the large areas of base colors (Russian: *sankir*; Greek: *proplasmos*) to each area of the icon. Usually he built up the heavier colors in several applications of thin color, allowing the bright white of the gesso to shine through the final painted surface, imparting luminosity and transparency to the colors. Here Ouspensky paid close attention to the way each color worked with the adjacent colors, and with the overall palette. He would tell his students to "Observe the material of the colors closely," which I understood to mean "The quality of the paint." For him, it was not enough to use the correct color, canonically; rather, the quality of that color was something carefully and intensively developed or, as he put it, "found." Cool colors such as greens and blues tended, in his work, to be washy, transparent, with visible brush strokes. Warm colors—reds and browns—tended to be more opaque, to appear most beautiful. Here one should remember Ouspensky's directions to the students: "Study the old icons, they are the best teachers." Everything he taught his students could be verified by the ancient icons.

Once the base colors had been applied, the lines (Russian: *rospis'*; Greek: *grapsimata*) of the original drawing were reapplied, and again, the quality of the color and opacity were carefully considered. Once, a student in the Saturday class had applied black lines to the blue drapery in an icon of the Savior. The lines were very thick and heavy, opaque. He told the student, "These black lines should be strong but still somewhat fluid to harmonize with the underlying blue garment."

Next would come the lighter patches of color on the area of the flesh (Russian: *probelov*; Greek: *sarcomata*),

---

50 Ouspensky, *Theology of the Icon* Vol. 1, 9.

51 See Ouspensky, *The Meaning of Icons*, 55.

clothing, and architecture, and often the background color. These colors were usually thin; sometimes applied in thin, watery puddles, with very few brushstrokes showing, and at other times applied in somewhat transparent daubs of paint. In the years I studied with him, there was no fixed rule for this part of the process. In a long life of daily painting, one can observe differences from one icon to another regarding this varying procedure. These colors would be applied in several layers, with each layer lighter (containing more white pigment) than the one before it. Then came the final highlights of white (Russian: *ozhivki*; Greek: *psimithies)*, which might be very strong or rather subtle.

The icon was left to dry for a few weeks, and then the varnish was applied. Leonid Alexandrovich used the traditional linseed oil varnish (Russian: *olifa*), an oil varnish that can be very difficult to work with; this was something at which he excelled. He insisted that one had to be directly taught this demanding technique by one who knew it well, or the icon would be ruined—a fact attested to by many modern iconographers. This varnish permeates the entire paint surface, imparting translucence to the colors, often changing them dramatically. Ouspensky planned on this alteration of the colors, taking delight in the moment when he would pour the *olifa* over the surface of the icon (lying flat on a table) and watch the colors deepen and become strikingly richer.[52]

Although these are the essential steps that Leonid Alexandrovich followed as he painted an icon, at least during the years that I worked with him, it would be wrong to say that he was inflexible regarding the process. "There are no rules." He sometimes took the steps "out of order" when it would work out better to do so. He sometimes finished a small area of the icon, to determine how he would complete the rest of it.

In 1983, I happened to see the great icon of St Geneviève (plate 59) in his studio, only partially completed. Most of the figure of the saint was finished, the scenes in the border and the Deisis at the top had been begun, but everything was still in progress, and the background was a very transparent yellow wash of raw sienna, or yellow ochre. At the bottom of the inner panel there was a small patch of vibrantly bright red, between the saint's elbow and the raised border. Ouspensky was considering this as the overall background color. He was still "finding" the color. Would it be this bright red, or a golden yellow, or an ivory white, or even a light green? All these colors can be seen in numerous examples of

Byzantine and Russian icons, and even in many icons painted by Ouspensky himself. Putting her reading glasses on and looking at the red intently and close up, Lydia Alexandrevna said to me, "Red, I think, is the color it should be." As one can see in the finished icon, the red was finally decided upon and applied. Even after that selection, it took Ouspensky quite a while to find the correct color for the border. Several were tried and removed until he settled on the transparent golden green found on the finished icon before us today. He worked on this icon for almost two years. This long effort to find the best colors is not what people see when they look at the finished icon. They see the face of the saint, and recall her great deeds. All the artistic endeavor serves this purpose: to bring the beholder to St Geneviève.

Ouspensky once said to me, "Icon painting is so difficult to understand because it is so simple." This is an interesting statement and one that I believe takes us to the heart of his understanding of the icon. Having observed and experienced the struggles of painting an icon, I wondered, Why would he say that it is "simple"? Later, I realized that I had misunderstood what he was saying. He did not mean *simple* as *not difficult*. He meant *simple* in the sense of being *not complicated*. The icon is difficult to understand because of its utter *simplicity*. I believe Ouspensky showed, in his painting and in his writing, that the essential meaning of the icon is not an intellectual construct, but rather, an encounter. To stand before an icon is to encounter the person or the event that is portrayed in the icon—the Savior, the Mother of God, an angel, a saint, a feast. The icon serves to facilitate that encounter—it acts as a catalyst for the encounter. It is a face-to-face, personal meeting of the subject of the icon and the person who stands before that icon. This encounter is transforming. As Ouspensky wrote:

> In the icon, the Church recognized one of the means which can and must allow us to realize our calling, that is, to attain the likeness of our divine prototype, to accomplish in our life that which was revealed and transmitted to us by the God-Man. The saints are very few in number, but holiness is a task assigned to all men, and icons are placed everywhere to serve as examples of holiness, as a revelation of the holiness of the world to come, a plan and a project of the cosmic transfiguration.[53]

Schemamonk Patrick Doolan

---

52 See Ouspensky, *The Meaning of Icons*, 53–55 for a fuller explanation of his icon painting technique.

53 Ouspensky, *Theology of the Icon* Vol. 2 (Crestwood, NY: St Vladimir's Seminary Press, 1992), 193.

Select Bibliography

Cavarnos, Constantine. *St Nectarios of Aegina.* Modern Orthodox Saints, vol. 7. Belmont, MA: Institute for Byzantine and Modern Greek Studies, 1981.

Cavarnos, Constantine, and M. Zeldin. *St Seraphim of Sarov.* Modern Orthodox Saints, vol. 5. Belmont, MA: Institute for Byzantine and Modern Greek Studies, 1980.

The Complete Octoechos. Trans. Isaac Lambertsen. Liberty, TN: The Saint John of Kronstadt Press.

Gorodetzky, Nadejda. *St Tikhon of Zadonsk: Inspirer of Dostoevsky.* Crestwood, NY: St Vladimir's Seminary Press, 1976.

Grabar, Andre. *The Origins of Christian Iconography.* London: Routledge and Kegan Paul, 1969.

Kovalevsky, Pierre. *Saint Sergius and Russian Spirituality.* Crestwood, NY: St Vladimir's Seminary Press, 1976.

Makarios, Hieromonk of Simonos Petra. *The Synaxarion,* vols. 1–5. Ormylia: Holy Convent of the Annunciation of Our Lady, 1998–2001.

_____. *The Synaxarion (Le Synaxaire),* vols. 1–5. Thessalonica: Editions To Perivoli tis Panaghias, 1987–2005.

Mango, Cyril. *The Art of the Byzantine Empire 312–1453.* Toronto: Sources and Documents, 1986.

The Menaion, vols. 1–12. Trans. from the Greek by the Holy Transfiguration Monastery, Boston, MA, 2005.

Ouspensky, Leonid. *Theology of the Icon,* vols. 1 & 2. Crestwood, NY: St Vladimir's Seminary Press, 1992.

_____. "The Problem of the Iconostasis." *St Vladimir's Seminary Quarterly* 8.4 (1964): 186–218.

Ouspensky, Leonid, and Vladimir Lossky. *The Meaning of Icons.* Crestwood, NY: St Vladimir's Seminary Press, 1982.

The Oxford Companion to Art. Harold Osborne, ed. Oxford University Press, 1970.

Paulus Silentiarius. *Descriptio Sanctae Sophiae et Anbonis.* I. Sekker, ed. Bonn, 1837.

Sotomayor, M. "Sarcophagi, Early Christian," with bibliography, in Encyclopedia of the Early Church, vol. 2. A. Di Bernardino, ed. Oxford University Press, 1992.

Symeon Thessalonicensis. *De Sacro Templo.* Patrologia Graeca. J.-P. Migne, ed. col. 155, 305–362.

Velimirovic, St Nikolai. "The Icon of our Lord Jesus Christ Not-Made-With-Hands." *The Prologue from Ochrid, Part Three.* Birmingham, England: Lazarica Press, 1986.

Vernadsky, G. *A History of Russia.* New Haven, CT: Yale University Press, 1943.

Welles, C. Bradford. *The Excavations at Dura-Europos, Part II.* New Haven, CT: Dura-Europos Publications; distributed by J.J. Augustin Publishers, Locust Valley, NY, 1967.

Zander, Valentine. *St Seraphim of Sarov.* Crestwood, NY: St Vladimir's Seminary Press, 1975.

Complete List of Published Works by Leonid Ouspensky

FRENCH

L'Icône. Quelques mots sur sons sens dogmatique. Paris, 1948.

"L'icône orthodoxe." *Messager de l'exarchat du Patriarche russe en Europe occidentale* 2–3 (1950): 75–82.

L'Icône de la Nativité du Christ. Paris: Éditions orthodoxes, 1951.

"L'icône de l'Assomption." *Messager de l'exarchat du Patriarche russe en Europe occidentale* 15 (1953): 171–179; repris sous forme de brochure, Paris: Éditions orthodoxes, 1953.

"Peut-on représenter la résurrection du Christ?" *Messager de l'exarchat du Patriarche russe en Europe occidentale* 21 (1955): 7–8; repris dans *La Vie spirituelle* (1979): 204–206.

"Quelques considérations au sujet de l'iconographie de la Pentecôte." *Messager de l'exarchat du Patriarche russe en Europe occidentale* 33–34 (1960): 45–92.

Essai sur la théologie de l'icône dans l'Église orthodoxe. Éditions de l'Exarchat patriarcal russe en Europe occidentale: Paris, 1960.

"André Roublev." *Contacts* 12:32 (1960): 287–293.

"La question de l'iconostase." *Contacts* 16:46 (1964): 83–125.

"À propos d'un des sujets du futur préconcile: La question de l'art sacré." *Contacts* 18:53 (1966): 24–36.

"Les icônes pascales orthodoxes." *Bulletin orthodoxe,* nouvelle séries, 3–4 (1973); repris dans *La Vie spirituelle* (1979): 193–203.

"Quelques remarques à propos d'articles récents sur la procession du Saint-Esprit." *Bulletin orthodoxe,* nouvelle série, 5–7 (1973): 21–34.

Théologie de l'icône dans l'Église orthodoxe. Paris: Éd. du Cerf, 1980.

"Entretien avec Chantal Savinkoff." *La Messager orthodoxe* 92 (1983): 50–55.

Vers l'unité? Paris: YMCA-Press, 1987.

"L'image du Christ non faite de main d'homme." *La Messager orthodoxe* 112 (1989): 9–13.

"La matière dans l'art sacré." *La Messager orthodoxe* 112 (1989): 14–17 (in collaboration with Lydia Ouspensky).

GERMAN

Der Sinn der Ikonen. Bern and Olten: Urs Graf-Verlag, 1952 (in collaboration with Vladimir Lossky).

"Symbolik des orthodoxen Kirchengebäudes und der Ikone." In *Symbolik der Religionen,* vol. 10: E. Hammerschmidt, *Symbolik des orthodoxen und orientalische Christentum,* vol. 1. Stuttgart: Hiersemann, 1962, 53–90.

"Der Einheit entgegen?" *Orthodoxie heute* 12 (1989): 10–22.

"Über Werkstoffe in der Kirchenkunst." (Place and date of publication not identified.)

ENGLISH

The Meaning of Icons. 1st ed., Bern and Olten: Urs Graf-Verlag, 1952; repr., Boston: Boston Book and Art Shop, 1956; 2nd ed., Crestwood, NY: St Vladimir's Seminary Press, 1982; 3rd ed., Crestwood, NY: St Vladimir's Seminary Press, 1989 (with Vladimir Lossky).

Theology of the Icon. Crestwood, NY: St Vladimir's Seminary Press, 1978 (trans. of *Essai sur la théologie de l'icône dans l'Église orthodoxe,* Paris, 1960).

Theology of the Icon, vol 1. Crestwood, NY: St Vladimir's Seminary Press, 1992 (rev. trans. of *Essai sur la théologie de l'icône dans l'Église orthodoxe,* Paris, 1980).

Theology of the Icon, vol 2. Crestwood, NY: St Vladimir's Seminary Press, 1992 (trans. of *Théologie de l'icône dans l'Église orthodoxe,* Paris, 1980).

"Symbolism of the Church." *The Orthodox Ethos.* A.J. Philippou, ed. Oxford: Holywell, 153–168.

"The Icon and Its Significance." *Sourozh* (1981).

"Iconography of the Descent of the Holy Spirit." *St Vladimir's Seminary Quarterly* 31.4 (1987): 308–347.

"The Problem of the Iconostasis." *St Vladimir's Seminary Quarterly* 8.4 (1964): 186–218.

GREEK

Ἡ εἰκόνα (Λίγα λόγια γιὰ τὴ δογματικὴ ἔννοια της). Athens: ΑΣΤΗΡ, 1952.